Golden Retriever

What the Golden Retriever
Experts Know – That You Don't

© **Copyright 2019 by The Golden Retriever Circle - All rights reserved.**

The content contained within this book may not be reproduced, duplicated or transmitted without direct written permission from the author or the publisher.

Under no circumstances will any blame or legal responsibility be held against the publisher, or author, for any damages, reparation, or monetary loss due to the information contained within this book. Either directly or indirectly.

Legal Notice:

This book is copyright protected. This book is only for personal use. You cannot amend, distribute, sell, use, quote or paraphrase any part, or the content within this book, without the consent of the author or publisher.

Disclaimer Notice:

Please note the information contained within this document is for educational and entertainment purposes only. All effort has been executed to present accurate, up to date, and reliable, complete information. No warranties of any kind are declared or implied. Readers acknowledge that the author is not engaging in the rendering of legal, financial, medical or professional advice. The content within this book has been derived from various sources. Please consult a licensed professional before attempting any techniques outlined in this book.

By reading this document, the reader agrees that under no circumstances is the author responsible for any losses, direct or indirect, which are incurred as a result of the use of information contained within this document, including, but not limited to, — errors, omissions, or inaccuracies.

Table of Contents

MY GOLDEN RETRIEVER STORY – SCOOBY 1

INTRODUCTION 9
    OUR GOAL 11

CHAPTER ONE: BASIC BREED INFORMATION OF GOLDEN RETRIEVERS 13
    CHARACTERISTICS AND BEHAVIORS OF THE BREED 14
    PERSONALITY TRAITS 15
    TEMPERAMENT 16
    A BRIEF HISTORY OF THE GOLDEN RETRIEVER 17
    POPULARITY OF THE BREED 19

CHAPTER TWO: THREE DIFFERENT TYPES OF GOLDEN RETRIEVERS 21
    BRITISH GOLDEN RETRIEVERS 22
    CANADIAN GOLDEN RETRIEVERS 23
    AMERICAN GOLDEN RETRIEVER 23
    THE DIFFERENT COLORS OF GOLDEN RETRIEVERS 24
    CAN GOLDEN RETRIEVERS CHANGE COLOR OVER THE COURSE OF THEIR LIFETIME? 25

CHAPTER THREE: GOOD WAYS TO CARE FOR YOUR GOLDEN RETRIEVER AND KEEP IT HEALTHY 27
    SETTING UP 27
    FEEDING 29
    HANDLING 31
    WASHING 32
    CLEANING 33

>   CARING..34
>   DOG-PROOFING YOUR HOME 35
>   DIFFERENT STAGES OF A GOLDEN'S LIFE:..............................36
>   WAYS OF CARING FOR EACH STAGE....................................39

> **CHAPTER FOUR: ARE GOLDEN RETRIEVERS SMARTER THAN OTHER BREEDS? 41**
>   A COMPARISON OF GOLDEN RETRIEVERS TO OTHER BREEDS ... 41
>   SUITABLE ENVIRONMENT FOR GOLDEN RETRIEVERS 43
>   WHAT MAKES GOLDENS UNIQUE?...................................... 43
>   BEHAVIOR COMPARED TO OTHER BREEDS 45
>   HOW POPULAR ARE GOLDENS? 46
>   WHAT MAKES THEM SO POPULAR? 47
>   WHY SHOULD YOU HAVE A GOLDEN RETRIEVER IN YOUR FAMILY? 47
>   HUNTING AND WHY THEY ARE SUITABLE FOR RETRIEVING GAME 48
>   WHAT ELSE DO THEY RETRIEVE? 48

> **CHAPTER FIVE: DEALING WITH A DOG THAT WON'T EAT ANYTHING 51**
>   PROBABLE CAUSES OF NOT EATING 53
>   SOLUTIONS TO BRING BACK YOUR DOG'S APPETITE 60

> **CHAPTER SIX: CERTAIN FEARS AND PHOBIAS 67**
>   COMMON FEAR OR PHOBIAS.. 67

> **CHAPTER SEVEN: HELP YOUR DOG GET THROUGH FEAR 73**
>   GENETICS 73
>   UNDER SOCIALIZATION 74
>   PRENATAL ENVIRONMENT... 74

- CLASSICAL CONDITIONING.. 75
- FEAR OF CERTAIN TYPES OF PEOPLE..................................... 75
- ADOPTING A DOG FROM AN ABUSIVE ENVIRONMENT............. 76
- WHEN YOUR GOLDEN RETRIEVER IS SCARED 78
- GROWLING AND BARKING THEN RETREATING OUT OF FEAR.... 80
- BODY LANGUAGE AND FEAR.. 82
- CAUSES OF FEAR AND ANXIETY 83
- FEAR AND ANXIETY IN GOLDEN RETRIEVERS.......................... 84
- HOW TO PREVENT FEAR? 85

CHAPTER EIGHT: DEALING WITH AN ENERGETIC, BOSSY, AND BITE-Y GOLDEN RETRIEVER PUPPY 93

- REWARDING YOUR GOLDEN 94
- WEAR YOUR PUPPY OUT 95
- ARE GOLDENS AN ACTIVE BREED OF DOG?........................... 96
- HOW MUCH ENERGY IS TOO MUCH? 97
- COMMON CAUSES OF TOO MUCH ENERGY 98
- WAYS TO CURE THIS AND PREVENT THIS FROM GETTING WORSE 99
- HOW MUCH EXERCISE DOES A GOLDEN RETRIEVER NEED?... 100

CHAPTER NINE: DEALING WITH AN AGGRESSIVE GOLDEN RETRIEVER 103

- HOW TO SOLVE AND DEAL WITH AGGRESSION 104
- STRATEGIES AND TECHNIQUES TO DEAL WITH AGGRESSION... 107
- IS IT COMMON TO FIND AN AGGRESSIVE GOLDEN RETRIEVER? 109
- DIFFERENT TYPES OF AGGRESSION 110
- WAYS TO MEASURE AGGRESSION IN YOUR DOG.................. 110
- POSSIBLE CAUSES OF AGGRESSION 111

CHAPTER TEN: GOLDEN RETRIEVERS AND WEIGHT ISSUES 113
CAUSES OF WEIGHT GAIN IN GOLDEN RETRIEVERS.............. 113
HEALTH PROBLEMS ASSOCIATED TO WEIGHT GAIN.............. 119
DIET AND NUTRITION FOR A HEALTHY GOLDEN RETRIEVER.... 121
BEST TYPES OF EXERCISES FOR GOLDEN RETRIEVERS 124
FREQUENCY OF EXERCISES.. 128

CHAPTER ELEVEN: CANCER IN GOLDEN RETRIEVERS ... 131
HOW COMMON IS CANCER IN GOLDEN RETRIEVERS?........... 131
HOW TO PREVENT CANCER? 132
WHAT AGE DO GOLDEN RETRIEVERS GET CANCER? 135
SIGNS OF CANCER IN GOLDEN RETRIEVERS......................... 136
COMMON REASON FOR DEATH IN GOLDEN RETRIEVERS 139

CHAPTER TWELVE: GOLDEN RETRIEVERS AND WATER 143
BEHAVIOR CHARACTERISTICS THAT CAUSE THEM TO LOVE WATER 143
DANGER IN WATER... 144
ACTIVITIES TO DO WITH YOUR GOLDEN IN THE WATER......... 149

CHAPTER THIRTEEN: INCONTINENCE ISSUES 153
GOLDEN RETRIEVERS AND INCONTINENCE 153
CAUSES FOR URINARY INCONTINENCE 154
HOW TO DEAL WITH INCONTINENCE? 155
HOW TO MANAGE URINARY INCONTINENCE? 156
DOG DIAPERS 157
HOW TO USE DOG DIAPERS? 157
PROS AND CONS... 158

CHAPTER FOURTEEN: WAYS TO MENTALLY STIMULATE YOUR GOLDEN RETRIEVER... 160

BENEFITS OF MENTAL STIMULATION AND HOW DOES IT AFFECT YOUR DOG'S BRAIN? 160
DIFFERENT ACTIVITIES AND GAMES 164
ACTIVITIES 165
ALWAYS USE POSITIVE REINFORCEMENT 167
TOYS AND TREATS FOR DOGS 168
BRAIN GAMES 168
THE LONG-TERM BENEFITS OF MENTAL STIMULATION 169

CONCLUSION 171

ABOUT THE GOLDEN RETRIEVER CIRCLE 177

This book is dedicated to all golden retriever owners. Our mission is to help each and every owner to have a stronger relationship with their golden retriever.

YOUR FREE GIFTS!!!

As a big Thank You from us at The Golden Retriever Circle, take this **FREE Golden Retriever Training Cheat Sheet** and **Quick Golden Retriever Training Dos and Don'ts List!**

Visit the link below for more info!

goldenretrievercircle.com/free-gifts/

How would you like to get your next book or audiobook for FREE and get it before anyone else??

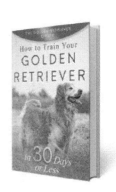

Audiobook

Receive your next book or audiobook (and future books) for free each time you leave a review!

Visit the link below for more info!

goldenretrievercircle.com/get-free-books/

LIKE AND FOLLOW OUR FACEBOOK PAGE!

facebook.com/grcircle

To receive the latest news and updates from The Golden Retriever Circle

And Also Join Our Facebook Community!

facebook.com/groups/grcircle

To Ask Questions, Discuss Topics, and Connect with Fellow Golden Retriever Owners

Be sure to check out our other books ***How to Train Your Golden Retriever in 30 Days or Less*** and ***33 Common Mistakes Golden Retriever Owners Make!***

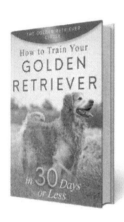

If you want to be known as the **"golden retriever expert"** among your friends and family, these books provide **proven strategies and techniques** to raise your golden retriever.

My Golden Retriever Story – Scooby

A foreword from Scott, one of the team members at The Golden Retriever Circle.

I remember clearly….it was the first week of November 1979 and I was around 5 years old at that time. The weather was getting really chilly at that time and the holiday season was kicking in. Christmas music was playing on the radio and relatives from out of town were calling us on the phone to coordinate plans for Thanksgiving and Christmas celebrations.

On one Saturday, a family friend had invited my parents, my two older sisters, and me to their home. We had gone to their home several times before but this time, there was something really different about this visit.

When we knocked on the front door, we heard some barking at the door. We had never heard barking whenever we had knocked on their door before. At that time, I remember being very frightened at the sound of barking dogs, so I hid behind my father. But when the door opened, much to my surprise, out came this excited dog to greet us.

I was still frightened since I wasn't used to being around dogs but this one kept on licking my face. It was a friendly dog and had this bright golden fur coat and a beaming smile on its face. It was a golden retriever!

Our family friend said that she and her husband decided to adopt this three-year-old golden retriever from the shelter after making a brief visit to the shelter. They said that they couldn't resist the glowing smile it had on its face and its cute personality, so they knew right off that bat that this was the right dog for their family. They named it Bella and were excited to take it home right away and surprise their kids.

We decided to stay indoors because it was really chilly outside and our mothers didn't want us kids to catch a cold and get sick. So, my two older sisters and I just played inside with their kids and Bella. We became really attached to Bella and thought she was the most adorable dog we had ever seen.

For the next few days after our visit to our family friend's home, we were talking about the golden retriever and wanted one really badly. Our home did not have any pets so my siblings and I really wanted to get a golden retriever like Bella. Weeks had passed and every time we saw our parents, we had tried to persuade them to get us a golden retriever like Bella. My parents did not really give us a definite answer but they always responded with hesitation, "Hmmmm…we will think about it."

My parents didn't seem too fond of the idea of having a dog in our small 1950s suburban ranch house. After all, they already had three kids to take care of plus all the busy responsibilities of an adult. A couple weeks had passed and deep down inside, my five-year-old-self along with my two older sisters were really disappointed. We realized that persuading our parents everyday did not really help turn the situation in our favor.

It was two weeks before Christmas, so our whole family

was in the middle of prepping for the Christmas holiday. One Saturday, our parents had left in the morning and said they were not going to be back until the evening. They told us that they will be going Christmas shopping. So that day, our grandmother was babysitting us.

Throughout the day, we were helping grandma with Christmas decorations inside of our home. When my parents got home that evening, my mother came inside, gathered us kids, and told us to wait in front of the door to the garage. They said that they had a surprise for us. I thought it was odd that they would be showing us our presents two weeks before Christmas.

My mother had opened the door, and in came a golden retriever! My sisters and I got so excited and started jumping up and down. It was wagging its tail and was barking with excitement to see his new owners. The dog had a huge smile on its face and was licking our faces with excitement. Our parents told us that they decided to adopt the one-year old (approximate age) golden retriever from an animal shelter after looking around town the whole day. They both thought having a new golden retriever would be a great addition to our fairly young family.

We were so overjoyed to start a new chapter of our lives with our new furry friend. It took us only a few minutes to unanimously agree on one name – which was "Scooby". It made sense to name our new dog "Scooby" since we religiously watched the cartoon *Scooby-Doo* whenever it would air on TV back in the 70s. The cartoon's main character Scooby Doo, which was a dog who helped solve mysteries, wasn't actually a golden retriever, but we named our golden retriever Scooby anyway.

Scooby felt like our youngest sibling…and also felt like our parents' youngest child. My parents really did their best to learn how to train Scooby. Overall, Scooby was a very sweet and loving dog but from time to time, he would exhibit some behaviors that would need to be changed. He would get excited whenever visitors by jumping on them and would not leave them alone. He even ran out several times whenever the door was open to socialize with the neighbors or greet the mailman.

It has been a while since my parents had raised a dog so our family friend (the one who owned Bella) had helped us train Scooby to follow simple commands and a few tricks. It took a while for us to ingrain those good behaviors into Scooby. After a couple of weeks, Scooby was not doing those undesirable behaviors as much as before.

Throughout our childhood, Scooby was a main part of our lives and an important member of our family. We pretended to be like the characters on *Scooby-Doo* and hunt for clues to solve pretend mysteries with Scooby. On some days, my mother would walk with the three of us siblings to elementary school and bring Scooby along on a leash. Scooby tagged along with us almost every weekend to go to the park or go to the lake.

After a couple of years, my father received a new job so our family moved to Columbus, Ohio. We moved into a larger two-story home with a much bigger yard. I was in middle school at that time and our family decided to adopt two golden retriever puppies: a boy named Maxwell and a girl named Lexi. They were both brother and sister and were both seven months old. Scooby was already turning eight years old but Scooby really loved to be around the younger pups. He treated them more like his own children, often being overprotective at times.

Our joyful home was filled with golden retrievers running around. My siblings and I had taken turns walking each of our three goldens and looking after their food. Scooby, even as an adult golden retriever, was as youthful as he was the day we first got him. Especially being around the two younger pups had helped Scooby stay youthful even into his old age.

When I moved out of our home to attend college back in 1992, Scooby was already 13 years old, a pretty old age in dog years! Scooby had passed away of old age a couple weeks after my freshman year in college began. It was sad to see Scooby go but we were all thankful that Scooby got to live a long life while being a large part of our lives.

Having Scooby as my first golden retriever (and first pet) really had a positive impact on me as well as on my family. I'd have to say that Scooby had ignited my interest in golden retrievers and dog training at a very early age. During my youth growing up in the 80s, I tried to get my hands on any dog training related book or VHS at my local library. I was just so fascinated with golden retrievers (and dogs in general) that I wanted to learn as much as I could about them.

Now fast forward to the present, I still have golden retrievers at home (two to be exact) and I love them to death. When I spend time with my goldens or when I see other dogs in public, it gives me that warm feeling back to when I was a child being with Scooby. Having a golden retriever can bring you and your family a lot of joy for many years! They are a great family dog to have and I wish you the best relationship you could ever have with your golden retriever.

Sincerely,
Scott

One of the team members of The Golden Retriever Circle

Introduction

We would like to thank you for choosing this book, *What the Experts Know About Golden Retrievers – That You Don't.* We hope you find this book informative in your quest to learn about one of the most loved breeds of dogs - the golden retriever.

You may have found this book because either you have just adopted or bought a new golden retriever. Or maybe you already own a goldie and need some help or want to improve on some areas of their behavior and habit. Or maybe you simply want to learn more information to help improve your relationship with your furry bundle of joy.

Whatever the reason is, if you are reading this book, you probably have or plan to get a golden retriever for your home. And why wouldn't you? They are among the most loved breed of dogs across the world. They have an amazingly friendly temperament and are a pure pleasure to look at.

Everyone knows how good-natured and easy to please a golden retriever usually is. This is why they make great companions and are also involved in different roles like service dogs for physically handicapped people, therapy dogs, and search and rescue dogs.

Golden retrievers tend to have a deeply embedded

devotion to the family they live with and you can depend on them to stay by your side until the end. Even on your worst days these little balls of fur can make you smile.

The way they take care of you in certain ways encourages you to have the same obligation towards them too. This is why it is important to learn about your dog as much as possible. You can learn what its needs and requirements are in this book along with an expert's guide on how to train the dog well.

When you first get your golden retriever, it can be a little frustrating to get him trained, but it is not impossible at all. Rescuing a golden retriever has never been a decision people regret. All the chapters in this book will help you cover the different areas that you may be concerned about.

Everything from the history of this breed to training them to fetch is given here. This book also covers many other in-depth topics on golden retrievers such as cancer in golden retriever, fears and phobias, and much more.

Training and understanding the retriever is just like getting used to a newborn child but fairly easier. If you just put in a little consistent time and effort, then you will have the perfect companion for yourself. No two dogs are exactly the same, but all golden retrievers have some common traits, and this will help you understand your dog.

Retrievers grow up fast and catch up quickly, so you need

to keep up your pace as well. You might have received a lot of advice from others, but it won't always work for you just because it worked for them.

However, you can put aside your worries and use this book to help you build a great relationship with your furry companion and take care of him as much as he takes care of you. This book was written after studying the behavior and temperament of golden retrievers.

Our Goal

Our goal here at The Golden Retriever Circle is to help you learn more about your golden retriever by giving you proven expert strategies and techniques to help you understand your golden retriever much better. It is our mission to help you the owner have a stronger relationship with your golden retriever, or any other dog that is in your life. Because we believe the bond between you and your dog is one of the most cherished and fulfilling relationships you could ever have.

There are many books and training resources out there being sold, but very few cater specifically toward golden retrievers. That is why we have taken the extra step to provide you with as much information pertaining specifically to goldens. After all, different breeds have different characteristics and behaviors, so we wanted to make sure that you are receiving the most relevant information for your own furry friend.

Within this book, you will find expert solutions to specific issues that you might encounter in your training journey. Unlike all of our other books *How to Train Your Golden Retriever in 30 Days or Less* and *33 Common Mistakes Golden Retriever Owners Make*, this book dives deeper into more specific issues that are not addressed in many general dog training books.

Our golden retriever experts have taken the time to compile a lot of this specific information into this one single book. This is so that you can save yourself a lot of time and not have to search for the answers. Without having this important information in this one source, you might get different sources telling you different and contradicting advice if you searched everything up yourself.

Keep in mind that a lot of the information in this book can also apply to other breeds of dogs as well. So, if you have any other dogs who are not golden retrievers, you can still benefit from the information in this book.

We would like to thank you again for choosing this book and we hope you learn a lot and get the best out of it. Now we know you must be eager to learn more things to help you train your furry friend. So, without any further ado, let's get started.

Chapter One: Basic Breed Information of Golden Retrievers

To help get you started off with the reading, we are going to cover the basic information about golden retrievers. The golden retriever, also known as the golden or goldie, is a well-balanced, medium-sized dog with a unique golden-colored coat of fur, ears which are small and drooping, and a tail that is at level with the body or sometimes has a slight curve which goes upward. The golden retriever is also a gun dog, which is a type of hunting dog used to assist hunters in locating and retrieving game.

Characteristics and Behaviors of the Breed

The golden retriever's most striking feature is its royal, shining, golden color. Another essential characteristic of the breed is its adaptability quotient. The golden retriever will adapt to a place if it gets sufficient amount of exercise as they show moderate activeness indoors.

But it is advisable to have a medium to a large yard at their disposal to get the best out of this breed. They are known to be very intelligent too and are ranked at #4 in the Dog Intelligence Ranking of the smartest dogs in the world.

Given their adaptability, training a golden retriever is particularly easy. But you need to be careful as they are sensitive and do not like to be treated harshly. Therefore, I do not recommend an excessive amount of strictness with this breed.

They are quick learners and extremely friendly which makes them perfect for jobs related to service or therapy. Golden retrievers can and will learn a number of tricks and have a tendency to remember what they are taught for the remainder of their lives.

With respect to shedding, the golden retriever does shed often, and you need to be prepared with a vacuum cleaner. Brushing at a regular interval will lead to a decreased amount of shedding and will result in a clean and soft coat. An occasional bath is sufficient to keep your golden retriever clean and looking their best.

Grooming sessions will help strengthen the bond between you and your golden retriever. They have nails that are strong and fast growing which need regular clipping or grinding to prevent cracking and splitting. A regular check up on the ears to see if there is any build of wax or other debris will help prevent infection, and regular brushing of the teeth is recommended.

Personality Traits

The golden retriever can be considered the classic companion for a family. Known for topping obedience classes, they often make podium finishes at dog sporting competitions. They are also known to be a very suitable breed for children and have proven to be very active, energetic, playful, affectionate, and protective of them.

Golden retrievers are also very friendly toward other breeds of dogs and are surprisingly very friendly toward cats as well. That being said, if you are a person who loves both cats and dogs, having a golden retriever and a cat in your house can turn out to be the most peaceful cat-dog relationship you will witness in your life.

Golden retrievers have been seen over the centuries as good watchdogs, but their doting love for people has termed them to be lousy guard dogs. Hunters consider them to be reliable bird dogs, and their strong sense of smell and passion to work with people makes them a desirable dog breed for any anti-narcotics team. To summarize, golden retrievers like to be around people and are very suitable for large and active families.

Temperament

Mostly all golden retrievers you come across will be friendly, well-behaved, and even-tempered. However, every owner should do a little bit of research about the breeder they plan to get their pup from. The popularity of golden retrievers has led to unethical breeding practices that have often resulted in puppies with temperaments that can be unstable in nature. All the training, exercise, and socialization in the world cannot undo a bad bloodline, and therefore it is very important to adopt from a reputed breeder.

The golden retriever is a breed that is very social and craves the companionship of people. Leaving them alone for too long without any exercise can result in the development of separation anxiety, which often ends up resulting in destructive chewing. A well-adjusted and grown golden retriever is a big chewer and therefore must be given sufficient chew toys and bones of its own.

If you fail to stimulate your golden retriever, it can run off with anything from shoes to books and other household items. They are very playful and like to play fetch and retrieve balls and other such items. Therefore, it is necessary to exercise them well with games like fetch to avoid any hyperactivity on their part. They are only occasional barkers and friendly toward strangers as well.

A Brief History of the Golden Retriever

Most of you may be aware of the interactive video game called Duck Hunt, which was popular in the 90s. You may remember seeing a disappointed dog that would show up every time you missed hitting a duck. The game relates to the history of golden retrievers and other such dogs.

The golden retriever comes down as a descendant of its predecessors who were bred back in the 1800s in Great Britain when sportsmen required efficient dogs to retrieve waterfowl, such as ducks and geese, and even for games on land. There is a record of the breed's origin, which is contained in a journal kept by Dudley Marjoribanks of Scotland between 1840 to 1890.

Dudley Marjoribanks had acquired a yellow pup, the only one from a litter of otherwise black retrievers, which were all wavy-coated. He named the pup Nous which means "Wisdom" in Greek. Nous grew up to be recognized as a golden and was bred with a Tweed Water Spaniel (which is now an extinct breed) resulting in the birth of a litter of four yellow puppies which were the foundation of the golden retriever breed.

Golden retrievers were largely unknown until 1904 when one of the dogs owned by the Marjoribanks won the first retriever field trials. It was then that the "Yellow Retrievers" were first registered with The Kennel Club of England as "Retrievers." A few years later, in 1913, goldens came to be recognized for their individual right as "Retrievers - Golden or Yellow".

Goldens first reached the United States in 1900 and became popular immediately. The first golden retriever was registered in 1925 by the American Kennel Club. Shortly after that, in 1938, the Golden Retriever Club of America was founded.

Popularity of the Breed

The trainability, grace, delightful, and calm temperament of the golden retriever contribute to the popularity of the breed as a suitable family companion. Goldens are people-pleasers and will learn all the tricks as fast as possible for rewards, praise, or some food treats. Therefore, the breed is an excellent choice for first-time dog owners.

Their quick learning abilities and affection toward people have made them the number-one choice for service and therapy dogs. In recent years, they have become a favorite of police forces who utilize them for sniffing drugs or bombs and for search-and-rescue operations. Given these characteristics, they are usually seen to be among the top 10 popular breeds in registrations at the American Kennel Club.

Chapter Two: Three Different Types of Golden Retrievers

In this section, you will learn about the different types of golden retrievers. You might have wondered if there is only a single type of golden retriever or if they come in varieties. You might have even seen different types of varieties of golden retrievers out in public or through pictures.

Well, the answer is that there are a few varieties that you can come across. There are essentially three main types: British, Canadian, and American; however, the differences between them are minimal and mostly cosmetic. Here is a brief look at each of them.

British Golden Retrievers

The British golden retrievers are also known as the English breed. The characteristic feature of these dogs is their long and feathery coat. They tend to be a little smaller in size compared to the Canadian golden retrievers. If you compare them to the American breed you will see that the differences are nearly non-existent. Their size, coat, and color will usually be quite similar.

The main difference, however, is in their build. The British dogs have a skull that is broader compared to the others and their forequarters are quite powerful as well. Another notable characteristic is their darker rim around eyes. Their muzzle will be well chiseled and balanced. The males of this type stand at 22-24 inches while the females are around 20-22 inches.

Canadian Golden Retrievers

The Canadian retrievers are a little different compared to the British and American golden retrievers. Their coat is not as feathery as the other two and their hair tends to be thinner and shorter as well. They usually stand at least 2 inches taller than the other varieties of golden retrievers, which makes them noticeably different. The males are usually 23-24 inches while females are 21.5-22.5 inches.

American Golden Retriever

Compared to the other two, American golden retrievers have a lankier build and are not as muscular. Their coat is long and feathery but darker than British golden retrievers. One characteristic difference is their lighter shade of eyes, which are more triangular in shape than round. The males tend to stand at 23-24 inches while the females are about 21.5-22.5 inches.

The differences in these varieties have actually emerged in a natural way over the course of their breeding.

The Different Colors of Golden Retrievers

Golden retrievers come in different shades and they all look amazing! Although their signature coat is golden, it can come in a variety of shades.

Their coat can come in light and pale shades as well as darker, rich shades. According to the standard, a purebred golden retriever will always have a coat in a single color. Their limbs and tail may have a lighter shade than the rest of the body but still similar. It is rare to see any mix of color like black or pure white with their golden coat. If there is any such characteristic, then the dog may be a mix of two breeds.

- The dark gold coat in golden retrievers is the most striking shade to be found.

- They may also be light gold which is usually a lighter shade than dark gold but darker than the color cream.

- The golden retrievers with a cream-colored coat are also quite popular and usually belong to the English variety. This is why this third color of the coat is found mostly in golden retrievers of the UK.

- Red golden retrievers are also quite striking, and this shade of coat also belongs to purebreds.

- Some golden retrievers have a beautiful white coat, but these are not a pure shade of white. The shade tends to be a light cream, which looks white under the light.

No matter what the color of their coat, remember to groom them well and keep their coat looking clean and shiny.

Can Golden Retrievers Change Color Over the Course of Their Lifetime?

Golden retriever puppies usually show their true coat

color after they reach the age of one. Notice the color at the tips of their ears. This is usually the shade that their entire coat will turn as they grow older. The feathering might be lighter for some compared to others.

The general observation is that a golden retriever coat will turn darker as they mature. A puppy tends to have light fur, so when the adult hair begins growing, you will notice that it is darker, and this will push the lighter hair inside as their undercoat. The puppy hair does not shed, and this is why golden retrievers will always have a double coat.

****

Before we wrap up this chapter......

Enjoying this book so far? Take a minute and leave an honest review. We would really appreciate your thoughts!

Reviews from awesome readers like you are very important for our books!

****

Chapter Three: Good Ways to Care for Your Golden Retriever and Keep It Healthy

If you have a golden retriever, then you need to take responsibility for it and ensure proper care. Taking good care of your golden retriever and constantly maintaining their health will help you out in the long run. Some of you might feel overwhelmed by the number of things to keep track of when maintaining your golden retriever's health and don't know where to start.

But don't worry. In this chapter, we will outline and explain the important things that you will need to get started with. The following are the steps you need to take in order to care for a golden retriever.

Setting up

Ensure that the house is safe for the puppy as well as an older dog. The steps to puppy-proof your house are given in another section. This will help you to create the right environment for your dog at home.

You also need to provide a separate place for it to sleep. It is fine to sleep with it in the bed, but there still must be a place specifically for your dog. For a puppy, you should try investing in a crate that will allow free movement for the puppy. Also, make a small dog lay down when it is tired.

Buy bowls for giving it food and water. Find ones that won't get knocked over too easily. There are many dog bowls available, which have additional grip on the bottom. They should also be of a material that it won't chew into too easily. The bowls should also be break-proof since dogs like to play with their bowls.

Contain your yard in a way that it won't run off while playing. You can set up a fence or just mark out one area for it to play. Also, install a tether so that it can go out for relieving itself.

While training a new golden retriever, it is important to get a collar, leash, and maybe a harness. This will help you take it on walks. Make sure the leash is long enough for it to run around freely even while you have a hold on it. Avoid putting a collar that puts too much pressure on the dog's neck.

Buy grooming supplies like a dog brush. You need to brush it regularly to avoid shedding all over the house. Also, get a nail clipper meant for dogs since their nails grow fast and you might get injured by mistake.

Feeding

Ask the veterinarian for recommendations on what food your dog should be fed. They will recommend food according to the age and health of your golden retriever. Puppies need to be fed food meant for them while mature retrievers will require adult food. There is also a different variety available for senior dogs. Find the highest quality of dog food possible and pay attention to the ingredients.

Use the chart to decide how much food you should be giving your dog. The age and weight will correspond with the amount of times it needs to be fed. Puppies generally need more food while adults require a little less. A growing puppy should be given three meals while you should stick to two meals for adults.

To bring novelty in their meals, try mixing a few added ingredients to the dry dog food. There are many healthy options available like chicken breast and plain and canned pumpkin. This will help it eat, especially in the case of a bad appetite. But too much of this will make your dog used to it and refuse to eat normal food.

Dog treats are great to use during training, but you should avoid excessive treating. It can be tempting to give it a treat every time your dog's cute eyes meet your eyes, but you need to control such instincts. Try giving a treat once a day for doing tricks or a simple command such as calling it to come to you. Dog biscuits and jerky are popular treats you should stock up on.

Make sure you keep refilling the water bowl and clean it well. Kibble might often fall into the bowl, so make sure to switch it out.

Handling

Pet your dog often and well. Remember to avoid touching its face, as it can be uncomfortable. Back up a little if you get too near to its face and it licks its lips or yawns.

Firmly but gently pat the sides of your dog. It will know that you want to play at that time, so remember to do this only when you really want to play.

Buy a few dog toys for it to play with. As retrievers, it is in its nature to play fetch. So buy some balls and chew toys that are safe to play with. It will be happy just with a simple rope but get a strong one that won't tear. Use games to teach commands to puppies and show that you are in charge.

Remember to teach simple commands as early as possible. Tricks are not that important but basics like 'sit', 'stay', and 'come' should be instantaneous for your dog. This will help in house training and help you keep it safe while going outside. It should obey these commands well before you go on walks outside in public areas. If you are not confident about training, then you can choose from the many classes and dog training facilities available.

Get your children used to playing with it in a safe and

friendly way. Don't startle a dog that has just come in since it might be frightened and bite. So teach kids to avoid any pulling and tugging until they are familiar with their new friend. It is easy to teach kids to play nicely in a way that won't hurt the dog in any way.

Washing

You don't have to give your golden retriever a complete bath every week or even every month; just give it a wash when it really gets dirty. For instance, it needs a wash after playing in puddles. You will also notice an unpleasant dog odor, so take the initiative for a bath at such times. Giving too many baths can actually cause skin issues for dogs.

Buy bath supplies like dog shampoo and keep towels specifically for using to dry your dog. Make sure you keep these ready to avoid a mess after giving it a bath. Avoid using human shampoo since some ingredients in human shampoo can harm it. Use dog shampoo to lather the whole body, but not the head or face.

You can use a common garden hose in the yard to give your dog a bath in the summer. If it is too cold out, use lukewarm water and the bathroom in the house.

After shampooing your golden retriever, you need to

ensure you dry him off well. Work into the fur to get all the shampoo cleaned off the undercoat as well. Soap residue can cause irritation on your dog's skin.

Towels will help you dry off the dog after a bath, but they won't be enough. Try using a blow dryer on cool setting to dry it off well. If it seems irritable towards the dryer, then just let it out in the sun.

Remember to use a brush after a bath so that no tangles are formed in the damp hair.

Cleaning

Just because it is a dog does not mean you don't have to clean their stuff. Take any blankets or sheets from the dog bed and put it out for a wash. Also, wash the stuffed toys it plays with. Remember to shake everything out in the open since you don't want fur in your washing machine.

Spot clean the dog bed if it cannot be put in the machine. Use a vacuum to clean all around the bed. There will generally be a lot of fur there. If you use a crate, then take it apart from the tray and wash it properly once in a while. Let it dry before putting it back in.

Caring

Use this book as a guide to care for your golden retriever well:

- Make sure to check over its body on a regular basis and look for any lumps or growths.

- If your dog flinches while touching any part of the body, then let the vet know as it might be a cause for concern.

- Ear infections are common in golden retrievers, so don't forget to look inside their ears. Bad odor from the ear is also a sign to look out for.

- Cut and groom its feet to ensure comfort. Check for any cracked foot pads and make sure the nails are never too long. Groomers can help you with this if you aren't comfortable with nail clippers.

- Pay attention to its movements to notice any abnormality. Stiffness or limping can happen due to a variety of reasons.

All of these steps will help you care for your golden retriever and keep it healthy. Don't take their health for granted and remember to feed and care for it every day.

Dog-Proofing Your Home

You know how there are certain changes you need to make in the house before a newborn child comes in? Well the same applies to a golden retriever puppy. Albeit, the changes and steps are different and less complicated, but dog-proofing your house is definitely a necessity. It will help you avoid many problems and aid you in training your puppy perfectly.

- Store all medication away so that your dog cannot reach them.

- Try to avoid smoking. If you do, then smoke away from them and keep the ashtrays in an inaccessible place. Store any pesticides, fungicides, or other toxic gardening material away from their reach.

- Keep your trash properly inside a container or in a place where they cannot play with it.

- Unplug electrical cords that are near the floor since they might bite into them. This is especially important when your golden retriever is a puppy.

- Keep your shoes away in the storage area so they cannot chew into them.

- Don't use any cockroach or rat poison in areas

that your dog might reach or play in.

- Don't use toilet bowl cleaners since they tend to drink from the toilet at times and cleaners can be toxic.

- Hide any antifreeze in the house.

- Certain plants, like Rhododendrons and Lily of the Valleys, are poisonous and should be kept away from their reach. They might bite into leaves of plants that are kept in the house.

- Keep things like yarn away as they like playing with it and might fiddle with your work.

- Keep an eye out for small objects, like coins and needles, that they might swallow and hurt themselves with.

- Store your socks away!

Just take these few, simple precautions and your home is ready for a golden puppy!

Different Stages of a Golden's Life:

You might not know this but a golden retriever's growth is affected by your handling and caring of it. Proper care will boost health and growth while the lack of it will affect it negatively. Keep in mind that different factors can affect the growth of the dog.

Change in diet often plays a big role in its growth. Your veterinarian can guide you in feeding it the right foods at the right age. Make sure to provide it good food that it enjoys eating so that its appetite is not reduced.

There are growth charts to help you assess the weight, height, and age of your dog at every stage. You can use these to compare the growth rate of your own golden retriever and look out for any abnormalities.

Although a golden retriever remains like a child mentally, its physical growth spurt is significant within the first year.

Right after birth, a golden retriever is usually blind and deaf. It is completely reliant on its mother at this point, so take care of them both. The mother will clean its puppies by licking and takes care of feeding them. The initial weight of a newborn puppy is usually about 14-16 ounces. This weight tends to double within 2 weeks.

The second week is when their eyes and ears start functioning properly. If you handle them in your hands, then keep them close to your body and keep them warm. Provide toys to play with while the puppy is growing and don't forget to keep grooming it.

The growth of your puppy has to be monitored carefully, especially around the 4th and 7th months after birth. Dysplasia is common in this breed, and you need to look out for signs of this that can occur due to rapid growth. Excessively rapid growth can increase the chances of injuries and even cancer.

Feed your dog kibble that is meant for large breeds that are low in calories. Follow a slow-growth plan given by the veterinarian. The weight gain should be steady and not more than 1-2 pounds each week. Regular exercise is essential to train it for good metabolism.

Golden retrievers tend to reach their full height at the end of the first year. It usually reaches around 24 inches when they stand. It will achieve its full weight by its second year. Males tend to be around 65-75 pounds while females are about 10 pounds lighter in comparison. Even as adults, their temperament remains the same as friendly young puppies. You will notice the difference and similarity when comparing a puppy greeting you at the door and an adult golden retriever jumping up on you.

Keep it active and well-exercised to avoid health risks and excessive weight gain. The more time you spend with it and take it out the healthier it will be. Plan frequent walks in the park or trips to the swimming pool or pond.

Around the 8_{th} year, your golden retriever will reach the stage of being considered as a senior. At this point, it will get a little lazier compared to before but will also remain just as loving.

Ways of Caring for Each Stage

Tips to care for a mother and her puppies:

- Let a puppy stay with its mother for the initial days or weeks. The mother will instinctively know what the puppy needs and will be able to care for it properly. Avoid separation during this time.

- You have to take responsibility for the proper health of the mother and puppy. Make sure that both are comfortable and well-fed. All nutritional demands should be met, especially right after birth.

- Provide clean water and food constantly to the mother as it nurses the babies.

- Make sure there is adequate space for them during the initial period and give them privacy. Keep this area quiet and ensure they aren't disturbed while resting.

- Take care of the proper vaccinations and take them in for regular checkups.

Chapter Four: Are Golden Retrievers Smarter Than Other Breeds?

We all know how friendly and loving golden retrievers are, but do you know how smart they are as well? Are they really one of smartest breeds of dogs? Actually, golden retrievers are ranked amongst the top 10 most intelligent dog breeds out there.

A Comparison of Golden Retrievers to Other Breeds

Let's compare golden retrievers with some other breeds now. If you haven't already brought one home, then you might be wondering if you should. It can be hard to choose a particular breed of dog since they all have their own attractive characteristics.

For instance, most people compare golden retrievers with Labradors, also known as Labs. These breeds have some similarities yet they are quite different from each other. Let us focus on the differences here.

Golden retrievers have slightly wavy coats, which are

water-repellent while a Lab has a more water-resistant coat. A retriever's snout is longer while Labs have a more medium-sized and non-tapered muzzle. Unlike golden retrievers, Labs can come in yellow-, black-, or chocolate-colored coats. Appearance-wise golden retrievers also have a friendlier and smiling facial expression, which makes them very popular.

As an example, let's compare golden retrievers to German shepherds. German shepherds are more athletic and protective but are comparatively cautious with new people. Golden retrievers tend to be friendly as soon as they meet someone unless they notice something off. Both of these breeds are very intelligent, but the golden retriever is a more family-friendly dog. If you are looking for more protection, then a German shepherd can be a more viable option.

A beagle is another friendly pet that is much smaller in size compared to a full-grown golden retriever. Their life expectancy can also be a little longer than golden retrievers. The cost of acquiring and feeding a beagle can also be smaller when compared to a more expensive golden retriever. Beagles have a lower tolerance for cold weather and higher tolerance for heat. Their coat is much shorter, but they shed more than golden retrievers.

There are many different breeds of dogs that you can compare your golden retriever too, but despite the pros and cons, it is hard to see your golden retriever in a negative light. These energy bundles are amongst the friendliest and most family-oriented dogs in the world, which explains why it is one of the most popular dog breeds out there.

Suitable Environment for Golden Retrievers

The thick, inner coat of golden retrievers makes them suitable for cold environments. Hot climates can be uncomfortable for them, so try to keep a golden retriever in a temperate climate. However, if the temperature falls below 45-degree Fahrenheit, then some golden retrievers will need extra protection.

They have the ability to adapt well to suburban and countryside areas. They love to wander, so you need to keep them in a fenced place. Breeders recommend that golden retrievers are given enough exercise on a daily basis. Some of them have a less-active nature and can be happy in urban apartments, but usually they are happier in rural areas where they have yards to run in.

What Makes Goldens Unique?

Golden retrievers are unique in so many ways, and all of

these traits make you appreciate this breed. Golden retrievers are actually a cross breed between Tweed Water Spaniels and Yellow Flat Coated Retrievers. This cross breeding was done in Scotland around the 1800s. Here is a recap of facts about goldens with some new ones as well:

- It was officially recognized as a breed by the AKC in 1925.

- As of 2018, according to the AKC (American Kennel Club), it is the third most popular breed of dog that people adopt in the U.S.

- It has a high tolerance for pain and can usually beat injuries which overwhelm some other breeds. This is why rescuers and law enforcement agencies often choose this breed.

- The color of its fur will darken with age and is similar to the color on the tips of its ears as a puppy.

- It has an amazing sense of smell that is superior to most other dogs.

- The webbed toes and the long tail of this breed make it easy to swim. Golden retrievers love playing in the water.

- It is also a great breed to choose for the purpose

of therapy.

- It has a double coat which sheds seasonally and is water repellent.

- It is extremely friendly with other animals and will learn to play well even if you keep a cat at home.

- It is extremely dependent on company and can suffer from depression if left in isolation too long.

- No matter how much you play with them or take them for a walk, they are always up for more. Their energy seems limitless when they see the opportunity to go out. They are also extremely curious and will always want to know what you are eating or drinking.

All of these facts make them unique and fun to keep around.

Behavior Compared to Other Breeds

In general, golden retrievers are very even-tempered and behave well when compared to other dogs. It is a social breed and loves companionship. If left alone, then this breed tends to develop separation anxiety. This can lead to destructive behavior, like chewing on shoes, cushions, or anything it has been taught not to play with.

If your dog is well-adjusted, then it just needs some chew toys to pass the time. It is easy to train golden retrievers as they live to please people. But this breed is also very sensitive and should be treated gently no matter what. It does not respond well to a harsh hand or tone.

It serves well as a watchdog, but if you want a proper guard dog, then this is not the breed to choose. Strangers will incite barking from golden retrievers but not violence. This will apply even if there's a thief in the house since it has a general affection for people. It has a keen sense of smell which makes it better suited as narcotic sniffers or bird dogs.

How Popular are Goldens?

Golden retrievers have been an extremely popular breed ever since they have existed. Their spot on the popularity list, as of 2018, falls at number three, according to the AKC.

One of the primary reasons that Labs are chosen more than them is because they require less breeding, while German shepherds come at number two because they make for great guard dogs and are also easy to train.

However, golden retrievers are still considered the best breed for large families.

What Makes Them So Popular?

The reason behind the popularity of this breed is evident in its temperament and behavior. It is friendly and intelligent. It also exhibits gentle behavior and is easy to train. It is full of energy and helps people stay energetic and happier in its company.

Why Should You Have a Golden Retriever in Your Family?

Golden retrievers are family-friendly dogs for various reasons. It is always eager to please and thus obeys well. It responds well to obedience training due to its pleasing disposition. It is also even-tempered and affectionate. The playful nature of this breed makes it perfect for kids. Despite being extremely energetic, they never display aggressive behavior.

Hunting and Why They Are Suitable for Retrieving Game

The golden retriever was bred as a gun dog originally. It got the name retriever in the first place because it could fetch any game, like duck or waterfowl, back without damaging it. The primary function and reason for breeding it was its non-slip ability to bring the game back to the hunter. This retrieving ability encourages it to play all kinds of fetch games well.

What Else Do They Retrieve?

Golden retrievers have the natural ability to fetch things

and can retrieve various things according to its training. It was primarily trained to fetch game, but no matter what you want your dog to fetch, you have to train it to do so. It will only do what it is taught. If you just throw a stick, then it will retrieve and play with it but not return it to you unless taught well. So, train your dog well and often and it will fetch whatever you want. It can become your personal, newspaper-delivery dog if taught well.

****

Before you continue reading…..

Liking our book so far? Feel free to leave an honest review for our book!

Reviews are super important for our books and we would really appreciate your thoughts on it!

****

Chapter Five: Dealing with a Dog That Won't Eat Anything

Golden retrievers, like other dogs, are usually big eaters. They will usually devour anything and everything you keep in front of them, without any hesitation. But then there can be days when your golden's appetite will decline, resulting in it keeping away from eating.

We once knew a woman named Marcy who owned a golden retriever named Mitch. Mitch was a very active and healthy three-year-old golden retriever who had played outdoors almost every day. He loved to explore the areas around their townhome and go on little adventures while Marcy was
gardening in her backyard.

He always had a good appetite and never had any history of diseases and illnesses. He was always fed the usual food, which was a dry food that was grain free. It seemed all of a sudden when Mitch started refusing to eat.

Marcy absolutely had no clue why Mitch had lost his appetite all of the sudden. Their daily routine didn't change however, Mitch did not look like he was feeling too well. Marcy had suspected that some strange contagious disease had entered into their home but Marcy herself was not sick. Perhaps, maybe Mitch's bag of dog food was a bad apple and needed to be returned to the store.

Marcy changed the type of food that he was eating and still nothing happened. He was still having no appetite and didn't want to eat. So out of desperation, Marcy took Mitch to the vet to have him examined. The vet had discovered that Mitch was having an upset stomach and gave some probable causes as to why this was happening.

However, it was up to Marcy to get to the bottom of this problem because she suspected that there was something in their home that had caused this illness in her dog for him to stop eating. If your dog is suffering from this problem of not eating anything, there are several probable causes that might contribute to this.

In this section, we will discuss the various causes why

your golden may not be eating and talk about solutions to get its appetite back on track.

Probable Causes of Not Eating

If your golden has lost its appetite, then it could be due to one of the following reasons:

Stomach Upset

If your golden has eaten something that it is not used to, then the snack in question could result in gastrointestinal problems, and it may require some time for the issue to subside. No matter how well-trained your golden is, there are chances that it will be tempted to gobble up bugs, trash, or objects that look like a treat to the eyes.

Eating inappropriate foods can lead to your golden experiencing some kind of stomach pains, and it will likely try to get rid of whatever it consumed. Like other dogs, they may try to eat grass or vomit. This can also end up in diarrhea. It can end up either way, and this might make your golden avoid food for some time.

Quality of Food

Food quality plays a huge role with golden retrievers, and

it will show in their reaction whether or not they are happy with the food. Food that is cheap often lacks an adequate level of quality ingredients and nutrients. It may end up having a low-count of protein that your golden may find to be unappetizing.

Also, the constant change in the type and quality of food will make your golden avoid it, especially if you have given them better food in the past.

Spoiled Food

Canine food is manufactured in a way to last a long time and have a good shelf life, but it can go bad as well. It is also difficult to determine the age of food and when it has become too old to eat. Food that is old can have mold growing in it, start smelling, and ultimately become unsavory for your golden. Furthermore, food that is old also loses the original nutritional value that is needed by your golden. Your golden will know when food has gone bad, and therefore it will try its best to avoid it. The chances of this happening to wet food is higher than that of dry food.

Overfeeding

Most owners like to reward their goldens with treats because they are so adorable and you feel like showing them love. It is tempting to pop a treat to your golden every time it flashes its cute, and literal, puppy face, but this may result in overfeeding. The amount of treats you give your golden should not exceed more than 10 percent of the total calorie intake of your golden in a given day. But this doesn't mean that you stop giving your golden treats altogether because that might affect their appetite too. On the other hand. giving too many treats can lead your golden into believing that it is their regular food, then they will lose interest in the actual food that you provide them.

Age

Your golden's body and senses will go through changes as they age. This may result in it occasionally rejecting food, and sometimes it may stop eating altogether. It may seem like the problem is associated with aging, but the cause could be something else that's simple and you may just not see it.

Maybe your golden has developed sensitive teeth and it's hurting because of age. Or there may be changes taking place in its senses due to age and the smell of the food that it is being given could become unappealing. If your golden is getting old, then care should be taken. You should give it food that is soft and has more flavor, so that you can lure it into eating.

Dental Problems

It is very common for canines to face dental issues, and your golden may suffer from them too. Since animals cannot express pain like a human, it may often go unnoticed.

If you see that your golden has gums that are swollen or bleeding, then it could imply serious issues which may get worse if not treated in time. Gingivitis and oral tumors may cause pain while chewing food. Broken or loose teeth can also cause serious pain in your golden with every single bite, which may lead to avoiding food and keeping away from chewing toys.

Medication and Vaccination

Healthcare for canines has improved a lot over the years. Advancement in medication and vaccinations has helped tackle various health issues and prevent dangerous diseases. However, these can lead to a few side effects as well. One such side effect is the loss of appetite. This is mostly temporary though. Your golden may lose its appetite for a day, but the effects will eventually wear off in a short amount of time.

Change in Routine

Your golden is a canine and it is habituated to a routine

by default. Once a schedule has been established, your golden will always stick to it. Introducing the smallest change in the routine can lead to discomfort for your golden. This includes a change in meal times or exercise time that can result in your golden feeling a bit of anxiety.

Changes can be made, but this should be a slow and gradual process. A sudden change in an everyday routine can result in your golden losing interest in eating until a regular routine is established again.

Being Choosy

Like us humans, your golden will have preferences too. It will be surprising to owners, but your golden will develop a taste toward specific food that it likes over time. It will enjoy certain flavors more than others that they may find repulsive. Ingredients that constitute the food matter a lot, and certain ingredients may cause your golden to avoid food. If this is the case, then you may need to find an alternative that your golden enjoys eating.

Feeling Bored

If you have been feeding your golden the same food from the same brand for years, then it may get bored of it. It can be that it used to enjoy it, but over the years it eventually got bored with it and has now begun to avoid it. Mixing a new flavor with regular food can be something to add variety to your golden's meals. Some wet food or gravy on top of dry food often works. It's also a good idea to switch food every once in a while, in order to keep eating interesting for your golden. This is so that you can avoid the possibility of your golden getting disinterested in food altogether.

Bad Habits

While switching the type of food or adding extra-flavored food every now and then is a great way to get your golden to eat again, it can also turn into a bad habit. Feeding human food to your golden is not the best thing for it. It may form a habit where it would demand human food more and not want to eat its dog food at all. Owners should sparingly give their dog human food or treats.

Medical Issue

The worst-case scenario where your golden is avoiding food is when it may be experiencing a significant illness. A common symptom of many illnesses is a loss of appetite. Although not eating food is not a clear indicator of what the illness may be, it is important to look for other symptoms.

Cancer, failure of an organ, and infections are serious illnesses which may result in your golden losing its appetite for a considerable amount of time if it is not treated. Also, if an illness is not treated on time, then it may lead to weight loss and an additional set of problems altogether.

Change in Environment

If you have moved into a new place or if you are on vacation with your golden, then it may show issues while coping with the change in environment. It may feel nervous and anxious in the new place, resulting in loss of appetite. Sometimes, even changing the location of their dish from one room to another can cause these issues.

Behavior Issues

There can be a variety of problems with respect to behavior that can result in your golden being hesitant to have a meal. These issues are often associated with past experiences.

For instance, if you have scolded your golden in the past while it was eating, then it may end up making it anxious during the next couple of meals. If you have adopted your golden from a shelter where it was used to eating alone, then it may take some time for it to get comfortable eating around people. These problems may seem difficult at first, but they can be fixed with some support and patience.

Solutions to Bring Back your Dog's Appetite

Since there are many reasons why your golden may have stopped eating, it can be a challenging task to take action and fix this problem. You do not want your golden to become unhealthy due to its loss of appetite, and there are several measures you may need to take to ensure its well-being. Establishing why your golden has stopped eating and making a change which will get them back to eating is what the responsibility of being a pet owner is all about. The following guidelines may help with getting your golden back to eating again:

Behavior Monitoring

You have to keep a constant watch on your golden's behavior. If they have skipped that first meal, then you have to start keeping an eye on their attitude toward food. Start making a note of their activities every day and crosscheck if that lines up with their regular, established routine. It is also not unusual for your golden to delay its meals by a few hours every once in a while. But if this is turning into a regular delay, then that is when you need to start getting worried.

Take note if you see a change in the pattern of their daily activities. Avoiding food can be just the beginning of other issues that may develop over the course of time. Anything that is not familiar should cause concern. It will be a good idea to monitor their stool and intake of water.

Environment Monitoring

You may have to play detective around your golden and investigate its surroundings. Try to understand if anything has changed in the past few days in the environment that might have caused a shift in your golden's behavior. If your golden has been around other people, then check with them if they noticed anything unusual as well. Your golden may have eaten something it shouldn't have, which may have led to a change in its behavior. Check if it got into your garbage bin by mistake and picked up something from there.

Examine the Body

As an owner, you can perform a basic, physical examination of your golden to see if you find anything unusual and determine if you need to go to a veterinarian. Brushing through the fur will help you find parasites, if any are present, and pressing your golden's belly will help you determine its firmness. The belly should usually be soft and not have any lumps. If your golden gives a reaction to the belly rubbing, then it may be experiencing some pain. Also, look for signs of vomit or diarrhea in the coat.

Examine the Teeth

After performing a body checkup, have a look at your golden's teeth. Make it open its mouth wide and do a simple, dental checkup. Look for any bleeding in the gums, if they are swollen, or if there are any teeth that may be loose. Also, check for any color change in the gum or accumulation of mucus.

Summoning the Vet

If you find that there is even a small issue, then it is always a good idea to call the vet. A veterinarian will be trained and able to perform a detailed examination along with any tests that will pinpoint the issue. They are skilled enough to determine any issue that may be causing pain to your golden for months, which will help you to make the necessary decisions early on in order to take care of it and potentially save its life from anything fatal.

Examine the Food

Irrespective of whether your golden is displaying any health issues or not, examining its food is always a good idea. Even a freshly-opened can may turn out to have mold or may be rancid. Start with smelling it for freshness. Even though dog food generally does not smell good, even if it is fresh, you will note if it has started going bad. It is also a good idea to keep an eye on the ingredients that constitute the food to ensure that your golden is not experiencing any allergy.

Change the Diet

After an examination with the vet and an examination of the food, you will sometimes be in a situation where you may need to change the diet. This can turn out to be the magical cure and restore your golden's appetite. However, ensure that you execute this slowly so as to prevent any sudden issues in regard to digestion. Mixing the new food with food that your golden is already familiar with is a good place to start.

Over the next few days, you can start reducing the old food and adding more of the new food until you make a complete switch. Even while making the switch, make a point of the nutritional content of the new food and try to keep it on par with the old food so that your golden always remains healthy.

Develop Good Habits

If the loss of appetite is caused due to issues in behavior, then the problem can be overcome by developing good, healthy habits and maintaining them. Decrease the amount of treats or human food you give to your golden so that it can get back to having its regular food. It is also important to give your golden its own, comfortable space to eat peacefully. Observe what routine is cherished by your golden and stick to it and ensure that it continues to eat every day.

If you are wondering what had happened to Marcy and her dog Mitch, it turned out that Mitch was eating a lot of cockroaches while everyone was asleep. Eating the cockroaches is what made Mitch very sick and lose his appetite. It made sense that Mitch would eat the cockroaches despite being an unpleasant snack because he had a huge appetite and would sometimes beg for more food after his meal portions.

A couple weeks prior to the whole dilemma, Marcy's home had several cockroaches running around the house, particularly in the kitchen area, close to where Mitch sleeps. Marcy had tried to kill each cockroach she saw and got rid of most of them.

After that visit to the vet, Marcy decided to diligently monitor the environment to see what could have been causing this loss of appetite. It didn't take too long to see that on one evening, she still saw several cockroaches running around the kitchen area.

They were gone for a few weeks and the dog was fine, however, it seemed that more of them would be coming out at night. So that is when the problems started because Mitch might have been eating more cockroaches than usual. But once they did a more thorough extermination of these cockroaches, Mitch was back to normal and eating again.

As an owner and good friend of your canine, it can be frustrating when your golden stops eating, but you need to keep your calm and patience. It is also important to be supportive as your golden is not just your pet, but family.

Chapter Six: Certain Fears and Phobias

Common Fear or Phobias

Let's list down the most common fear or phobias that a golden retriever might have.

Being Left Alone

We have established that golden retrievers adore people and love pleasing them. This means that they love the company and being around a family makes them really happy. The downside to this is that they have a fear of being left alone. Having no one at all around can result in your golden being upset or sad.

It may happen so that you may not be able to be around your golden all the time. Therefore, it is important to train it to be able to be by itself for at least short durations of time. Make yourself absent for smaller durations of time and eventually increasing it, which will teach your golden to be self-sufficient. Keep it occupied with toys and other things it loves, which can be done without the need of any human help.

The Veterinarian

It is normal for golden retriever pups to be scared of the veterinarian. A visit to the vet involves new smell, new people, being handled or touched in new ways and getting restrained to some limit too, and not to forget, vaccinations. So, it's no surprise if your golden is scared of the vet.

This can be fixed easily. You can take your golden to the vet just for socialization, which involves no checkups. This will make your golden familiar with the people and smells at the veterinarian's clinic and it will eventually become comfortable with the visits.

Car Rides

The lack of exposure to car rides in the earlier years of your golden's life can lead to the fear of car rides. It can also be due to negative experiences in a car ride when the ride is always to the veterinarian, or to be left at a shelter home. Or maybe your golden has gotten sick during the previous car rides.

You can use treats to lure your golden into car rides and praising it every time it musters the courage to get into the car. You can start with small car rides to places that your golden loves such as the park where you play with it. This will make your golden fall in love with car rides and it will eventually get over its fear.

Staircases

As an owner, you may fail to notice your golden's fear of stairs until it actually stops or hesitates its movement while approaching a staircase. This phobia can easily develop as a result of a lack of early socialization to staircases. If your golden retriever pup never experienced a staircase while growing up, it may end up fearing them after it grows up due to lack of exposure.

Most of the time you can get rid of this fear by turning going up and down the staircase into a game. Rewarding every time your golden makes it through will only encourage it and help it get over its fear. While other times, some goldens may not be able to make it through the entire staircase in one go and will only get over their fear by going through one step at a time.

Thundering

The fear of thunder is known as Astraphobia and it can be common in a golden retriever pup. The level of this phobia differs from one dog to another. While some goldens may have a fear of thunder that is very mild, others might tremble and tuck their tail between their hinds or run and lose control and hide somewhere.

Extreme fear can result in your golden getting destructive and even losing bladder control at times. Dogs are usually also able to sense a thunderstorm coming before humans can and therefore there are cases where you may see your golden running around the house suggesting about an incoming thunderstorm.

Holding your golden close to you and comforting it will help most of the time during thundering and lightning. You need to give it assurance that you are there to take care of it and will nothing happen to it.

Fireworks

Fear of fireworks is another phobia that is common. It is very similar to thunderstorms as the unpredictable show of lights and noise can end up making your golden tremble in fear.

In most cases, slowly trying to get your golden used to

the noise of fireworks will do the trick. In other cases where your golden may be extremely scared, you may need to get a veterinarian involved who will try to calm your golden down with medication and sedatives.

Strangers

This fear is associated again with the lack of socialization to enough people during the growing up process. It is important not to impose meeting strangers on to your golden. Let it take its own time. Also, as we have discussed earlier in detail, pairing up a stranger with something your golden loves is one approach that can be taken to bridge the gap between the golden and strangers.

Children

Your golden can fear children for various reasons. Again, lack of socialization and not being used to having children around them in an early age can result in anxiety around kids. It is extremely common for people to get dogs before having children. If you get a puppy before and then suddenly introduce children to it when it grows up or when it is older, your golden may not get the chance to socialize with the children.

There are some chances of your golden having a negative experience with children. While children usually mean no harm to a pup or a dog, it could be interpreted by the golden as a threat. Consulting a trainer is the best thing to do to work on this phobia for the betterment of both your golden and the children.

Household Objects

There are chances that your golden may develop a fear toward specific objects in the house: decorations, vacuum cleaner, or toys belonging to children. Usually, this is not a big deal as the easiest thing to do is keep the object out of sight from your golden. However, sometimes, this can be troublesome. For example, if your golden trembles every time you take your vacuum cleaner out, you may need to slowly introduce it to objects it is scared of in a happy and positive manner.

****

Before you go further.......

If you are finding our book helpful to you, feel free to take a minute to leave an honest review!

We would really appreciate your thoughts on it since reviews are very important for our books!

****

Chapter Seven: Help your Dog Get Through Fear

Golden retrievers are generally a happy breed and can adapt to almost anyone and anywhere, but we cannot completely disregard the fact that it is still a living being and can have its own share of fears. There are several factors that can contribute to a golden being scared or fearful of certain things or other dogs or even people. Let's discuss the most common reasons.

Genetics

Your golden might be fearful or scared as a result of inheriting genes from either or both of the parents who have experienced some kind of fear during their lifecycle.

We have also discussed earlier how breeding plays an important role and how the popularity of golden retrievers has led to unethical breeding practices that again can play a big role in the gene pool of the newly born litter.

Under Socialization

Golden retrievers are truly fond of people and it is important to introduce them to all kinds of people from their puppy days. If you miss the boat of socialization in the golden's early days, it can become fearful and depressed as a result of a poor history with respect to socialization.

Prenatal Environment

Fearfulness can also be instilled in a golden retriever if the mother went through stress during pregnancy. Therefore again research about the breeder and how well they take care of the mother during pregnancy is something to look at before adopting a golden.

Classical Conditioning

Some goldens, like most dogs, can associate fear of certain objects or activities. For example, some goldens are scared of nail clippers and associate it to something negative. So, whenever you pull out a nail clipper, it will be bad news for them, and you will need to find ways to get them over the fear of such activities that are routine for them.

Resolving fearfulness in a golden can be a slow process as compared to fixing problems like not coming when being called, pulling the leash or rowdiness. This is because fear is associated with emotional response and does not fit in the domain of problems, which are associated with obedience. So, the approach here will have to be much different than that when you are trying to instill manners in your golden.

Fear of Certain Types of People

We have spoken about how golden retrievers adore people but there can be instances wherein they are scared of people. Consider you are walking through the park with your golden one morning as usual. There is a person walking toward you and as the person comes closer, you see your golden disappearing into the bushes behind you.

You look behind and you see it in an almost paralyzed state and wonder why it would be scared of a regular human being.

The approach to solve this issue is to create a positive response to the thing that your golden is scared of. In this case, it is a stranger and a simple but useful approach that has worked most of the times is pairing the thing your golden is scared of with something that it loves the most.

Since your golden is scared of strangers, let the stranger feed him his most favorite treat that makes it the happiest dog in the world. The strategy here is to make it feel that the treat appears whenever strangers appear and the treat disappears when the strangers are gone, ultimately making it believe that having strangers around is a good thing.

Adopting a Dog from an Abusive Environment

Animals usually do not have bad intentions at heart but unfortunately; we cannot say the same about humans. And therefore, there are chances that an unfortunate golden landed up in an abusive environment that changed its idea about humans forever. It could have been in an environment where the golden was abused verbally or physically. Verbal abuse leads to emotional imbalance and physical abuse can lead to worse. There are owners who abuse their dogs or don't feed them and take proper care of them. These goldens would end up abandoned most of the times and would need to be rescued by organizations that work for animal welfare.

If you have considered adopting a golden who lived in an abusive environment before, it would take a lot of effort to win its trust over as a human again. Goldens are generally people-lovers and when their trust has been broken by a human with abuse over the years or especially from the time when it was a puppy, it would leave a golden broken in spirit. You will need to handle such a golden with utmost care and love to make it believe in people again.

It might scream or cry if you pick it up or try to pet it. The good news is a golden has unconditional love, and although it may take time, it will start loving a human again because it is naturally fond of people. In such cases, give it space and time. Feed it well and eventually it will realize that you mean no harm to it.

One day at a time and you will start closing the gap that it has built between itself and people. Seeing the warmth and nurturing you provide, it will start getting close to you gradually. The trick is not to impose yourself on it and let it take its time.

Also, given that we have established that goldens adore people and are people-pleasers, they can always be rehabilitated. Some goldens may exhibit aggressive behavior. They also may be unresponsive to people based on the trauma that they have been through. They may be quiet and not willing to come close or play but usually goldens are not associated with aggressive or violent behavior, simply because of the fact that they are known to love companionship.

When Your Golden Retriever Is Scared

There can be a time when a golden gets so scared that it will shut down physically or almost go completely limp. It is important to analyze the reasons that are causing this behavior and take appropriate measures to make it feel comfortable.

You need to ask yourself the following question, which will help analyze the cause of the fear and the situation.

1. Do you know of an event or a timeline since the fear started?

2. Is the thing that your golden fears actually going to cause it any hurt or pain? If yes, how will you intend to keep your golden safe?

3. Are other people or animals around your golden at risk because of its behavior due to its fear? If yes, how do you plan to control the situation?

4. How do you intend to keep your golden comfortable and safe when it is experiencing fear while you work on steps and measures to modify its behavior?

5. Is it absolutely necessary for the golden to get over this situation and cope with it or will it go away just by keeping it away from the situation moving forward?

6. Is it more practical to protect your golden from this situation than just trying to treat the fear? If yes, give it some time to get used to your plan and chances are that it might end up becoming happier than before anyway.

The answers to these questions will help you identify the fear and then you can deploy steps for conditioning your golden to resolve its fear. Conditioning implies helping your golden get over the fear or teaching it to live with the fear by recreating or introducing the fear in small quantities. Doing this will ultimately make it feel that there is nothing to fear.

The approach is to start at a distance with low intensity for a short period of time. This will help you understand your golden's threshold for the fear and at what point it feels safe. Next, plan on how you will gradually decrease this distance and increase the intensity over a longer exposure of time. The variable of time should be gradually increased at every step. And after every iteration of this exercise, don't forget to praise your golden in a high tone, which will make it feel rewarded.

Growling and Barking Then Retreating Out of Fear

Growling or barking occasionally is a golden's way of letting you know that they may be frightened, hurting, confused, upset, or sad. A growl with a quick bark does not always imply aggression or anger, but it could be your furry friend's way of seeking attention to try to let you know that something is wrong. It can also be that the golden is trying to interact and communicate to inform you that it needs attention, namely for activities like potty, or that it's thirsty, hungry, or bored.

If it is the first time that you are observing this kind of behavior, it would be advisable to get in touch with a vet or an experienced golden retriever owner who could elaborate more about the situation.

Golden retriever puppies are like toddlers. They have very limited experiences and their brains are not fully developed and they are still learning to live their role in life. They need attention, training, kindness, and patience, irrespective of the reason for their growls or barks.

Body Language and Fear

Golden retrievers (and all dogs as well) have an elaborate and distinctive second language that shows exactly how they are feeling without using any sound, which they convey using their facial expressions and holding their body in various postures. You just need to learn how to decipher this body language to understand them better. And when you will finally learn to read this body language of a golden retriever, it will gift you with the special ability to understand and tend to their needs.

Learning their body language will also help you to change your behavior and mood to suit their needs. This will make you an attentive owner in the eyes of your golden and the bond between you and your golden will only get stronger as this will help you communicate with each other more effectively.

A frightened or a scared golden will make itself look smaller in size, which is a submissive strategy so that they don't look threatening and invite any kind of attack. They will crouch low, touch their head to the ground, narrow their eyes, the ears will be pinned behind, and they will be half-turned, looking away from whatever scares them. But they will take frequent glimpses of the thing that they are scared of.

The biggest sign of fear would be their tail, which will be

low and tucked between their hinds, under the body. The weight is shifted more on the lower body so that that can jump and run away. This is the body language through which a golden will exhibit fear and every owner must know about it to take care of the golden and make it feel safe.

Causes of Fear and Anxiety

An ideal golden retriever will not be prone to fear or anxiety as much as other dog breeds. However, there are factors that we cannot rule out wherein fear and anxiety come into effect much for the same reasons a human child would be fearful or anxious. As discussed earlier, golden retriever pups are much like toddlers and the cause of their fear and anxiety can be narrowed down to the following 3 reasons.

Separation

If you have adopted a golden, which was rescued after separation from a previous owner under any circumstances, it could be prone to separation anxiety. It will always be scared that you might leave it too or you may end up separating from it again. You have to be there for your golden as much as possible in this case and build a trustworthy relationship, which will make the golden believe that you will have its back at all times and will never leave it.

Loud Noises

Loud noises from fireworks, thunderstorms, construction sites or even everyday household items like vacuum cleaners can tend to scare a golden retriever.

Social Situations

If the golden had lack of socialization as a pup, it could lead to anxiety while facing new people or animals. As discussed in one of the previous chapters, this can be tackled by introducing the golden to strangers or animals they are scared of over a small period of time and then increasing the time window slowly and gradually.

Fear and Anxiety in Golden Retrievers

Golden retrievers are known to be friendly and happy right from birth and therefore, you will not get to see fear and anxiety as a common display of behavior in golden retrievers. Given that most goldens are cheerful, the odds of fear and anxiety being passed down to a litter are really low. However, if the parents have had a history of trauma or ill treatment, there is a small chance that this may get passed down in the gene pool. Research and selection of the breeder, therefore, plays an important role.

How to Prevent Fear?

Follow these 4 simple steps to prevent fear in your golden retriever.

Investigate the Trigger Causing the Fear

The primary step is to understand what is causing the fear or anxiety in your golden retriever. It can be obvious at times and sometimes it can be a riddle that will take quite some time to be solved. If your golden is just barking at another dog across the street, it is obvious that the trigger is the other dog. And when it is a riddle, the trick is to pay attention to your golden's body language.

We have learned how body language can fill the communication barrier between an owner and their golden. Is your golden continuously staring at something? Is it running in the opposite direction from something or someone? If you still can't figure it out, it is always advisable to seek help from a vet or a professional.

Remove the Trigger from the Equation

Removing the trigger initially will just prove to be good for the well-being of your golden. Higher exposure to the trigger can lead to a higher amount of stress and anxiety. Therefore, once the trigger has been established, try to avoid it as much as you can until you have charted out a plan to help your golden get over the fear.

Do not use Force with your Golden to Confront the Fear

It's natural to think that if you force the item of fear on to your golden, it will eventually give in and get over the fear. But dogs do not work that way. If you end up forcing your golden into something that makes it stressed or anxious, then chances are that those feelings may escalate, and your golden will become aggressive to the fear. It may transform into your golden attacking you or attacking the person or object that is causing the stress.

Training to Get over the Fear

Training is what will ultimately help your golden get over its fears. There are several approaches to it as we have discussed earlier and the method to be chosen will be subject to the kind of fear in concern.

YOUR FREE GIFTS!!!

As a big Thank You from us at The Golden Retriever Circle, take this **FREE Golden Retriever Training Cheat Sheet** and **Quick Golden Retriever Training Dos and Don'ts List!**

Visit the link below for more info!

goldenretrievercircle.com/free-gifts/

How would you like to get your next book or audiobook for FREE and get it before anyone else??

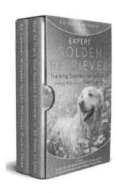  

Audiobook

Receive your next book or audiobook (and future books) for free each time you leave a review!

Visit the link below for more info!

goldenretrievercircle.com/get-free-books/

LIKE AND FOLLOW OUR FACEBOOK PAGE!

facebook.com/grcircle

To receive the latest news and updates from The Golden Retriever Circle

And Also Join Our Facebook Community!

facebook.com/groups/grcircle

To Ask Questions, Discuss Topics, and Connect with Fellow Golden Retriever Owners

Be sure to check out our other books ***How to Train Your Golden Retriever in 30 Days or Less*** and ***33 Common Mistakes Golden Retriever Owners Make!***

If you want to be known as the **"golden retriever expert"** among your friends and family, these books provide **proven strategies and techniques** to raise your golden retriever.

Chapter Eight: Dealing with an Energetic, Bossy, and Bite-y Golden Retriever Puppy

Golden retriever puppies can get really hard to control at times. When they want attention from you, they may jump on you and bite you not with the attention of hurting you but to really just get your attention. There are times when golden puppies will be so full of energy that they will go crazy in the living room and may misbehave.

If you try to calm them down, they will run away from you and then suddenly appear after some time. They will bark and simply not pay heed to what you have to say. This may turn out to be the most difficult time as your golden puppy is at an adolescent age and the following tips may come handy to absorb all the energy that furry little bundle has inside it.

Rewarding your Golden

Make sure that you are not rewarding your golden puppy for every single activity it does. You will also need to establish and lay down what rewarding actually means. Also, educate other members in your family to not reward your pup for activities that you want to avoid in the house. Always keep regular intervals of time between rewarding your pup, which can be treated as a rest period. This will help your pup to not associate rewarding with activities that are not desirable by you.

What does your Pup Really Want?

Try to understand what is it that your golden pup really wants - toys, food or just play time, etc. Try to channel the energy into these things that it wants and then you can reward it for something that you believe is worth rewarding. Try to deviate your puppy's attention from jumping on you to something like fetching a toy and getting it back to you and conditioning it to keep all four legs on the ground while doing so.

Wear your Puppy Out

Sometimes it is a good idea to wear your golden puppy out in the mornings. You can also combine this effort with long walks, runs, training, and other exercises which will really wear your golden puppy out. Doing this will help it to be calm during the remainder of the day. When your puppy is calm, do not encourage any more activities and convert this calm time into a routine.

In a few days, this will be very natural where you will take your puppy for walks or exercise in the mornings and then it will be calm for the rest of the day. This can be a challenging task while dealing with golden puppies, but it's good to develop a routine at an early stage and it's natural for canines to work on an activity in the early morning than in the evening.

Are Goldens an Active Breed of Dog?

Golden retrievers are indeed an active breed of dogs. They are a breed of working retrievers. It implies that they have a very high level of energy, which needs to be utilized for productive activities. Failing to release this energy for productive activities will result in its utilization for activities that are less desirable for you such as jumping around, being hyperactive, and just chewing on objects at home such as furniture.

While golden retrievers come across as a breed that only wants to cuddle and give kisses or just snuggle on the couch, a majority of golden retrievers are a high bundle of energy. They will settle down for the day only after they have received their daily dose of walks, training on obedience, and games like fetch.

Let's also try to understand that every dog is different and not all golden retrievers have energy that is uncontrollable. There will be some that will exhibit a lot of energy throughout their life and some will be calm even as small puppies.

How Much Energy is Too Much?

Golden retrievers are bred to be working retrievers. So it is really normal for them to have a lot of energy in them. The traits that are sought after in golden retrievers are high energy and stamina so that they are active all the time. These traits have given golden retrievers the energy to go all day long, running in the fields for miles and miles without having the need to take a break.

Common Causes of Too Much Energy

The golden retriever is a breed for sport and was created to retrieve fallen birds for hunters in the highlands of Scotland during the 19th century. The Scottish Highlands are full of mountainous terrain with pot-holed ponds, streams, lakes, etc. and retrieving anything from this kind of terrain is a physically challenging task.

So when the golden retriever was in mind of breeders, the idea was to have a breed that would be full of energy and have a lot of stamina with a liking toward water. The idea was to have a dog, which would not get tired of going the distance, swimming and hiking through rough and difficult terrain for the peak hours of a full day. And that is exactly what was achieved with the golden retriever.

One might argue that as a pet for the family, a golden retriever is not required to do such heavy work, but you cannot disregard the fact that they have the genetics, which are tailored for the role they were originally created for. Therefore, they have a mind and body, which is created for tough activity and hence, if they lack sufficient exercise, the result that you get is highly not what you would desire as an owner.

A lot of owners complain that their golden retriever is out of control. No, it is not out of control, but simply hasn't been given enough exercise. The golden has just not met its basic needs of exercise to release its bundle of energy as a result of which it is just jumping and bouncing on the walls to just burn all that stored energy.

Ways to Cure This and Prevent This from Getting Worse

Having too much energy is natural in golden retrievers and should not be treated as a negative thing. What you need to work on as an owner instead is how to control this energy and channel it in the right direction. The best way to do this is by giving your golden retriever a sufficient amount of exercise.

How Much Exercise Does a Golden Retriever Need?

A good thumb rule for golden retrievers to establish how much exercise is needed is to deploy the '5-minute rule'. This rule basically states that a golden retriever should need 5 minutes of exercise for every month it's been alive. For example, if your golden retriever pup is 3 months old, it should be given 5 minutes x 3 months which is equal to 15 minutes of exercise every day. If your pup is 5 months old, it should be given 25 minutes of exercise every day.

The exercise should be a structured exercise. It should be a walk while on a leash or a game involving fetch. It should be an addition to general playtime and not a substitution for it. Golden retriever puppies have all the energy in the world to go on and on, but you need to be careful not to exercise them too much.

Puppies are in their growing phase and over-exercising can lead to bone or joint damage. So, as an owner, you need to take it slow and easy until your golden has matured. The 5-minute rule is the best and simplest approach while encouraging very little jumping. You can continue with the 5-minute rule until your golden turns a year old.

As an adult, a golden retriever needs an hour of exercise every day. But you can increase or decrease this time based on the genetics of your golden retriever. There is no hard-encoded rule for this but an hour's exercise every day is a good place to start and you can boost it further if required. All golden retrievers need regular exercise.

Try to have at least two rounds of exercise per day with your grown-up dog, which they may tend to get destructive. You can try different types of activities such as swimming, hiking, running, etc. Remember that stimulating the heart and the muscles is as important as stimulating the mind.

Also, remember that there is no need to worry about giving too much exercise to a healthy adult golden retriever. They tend to take every bit of challenge you throw at them and are capable of doing much more. You will get tired but a golden might not get as tired as you.

****
Before you go ahead……

If you are enjoying our book so far, don't forget to take a minute and leave an honest review!

Reviews from awesome readers like you are important for our books so we would really appreciate your thoughts on the book!

****

Chapter Nine: Dealing with an Aggressive Golden Retriever

Golden retrievers are people lovers and people pleasers and it is very rare that you may come across an aggressive golden, but it can happen, and you cannot disregard this possibility. Goldens are very intelligent and training and educating them is easier compared to other breeds.

Poor breeding can give birth to an aggressive golden puppy and it is necessary to deal with aggression issues as fast as possible because aggression in golden retrievers can grow over time if it is not treated at the right time.

Aggressiveness in a golden retriever puppy can start at an early age of 6 weeks as they may be weaning while they are parting from the breeder. Therefore, it is important to adopt your golden from a trusted breeder. You should also try and meet the parents of the puppy to see if they have any issues with respect to behavior. You should always make it a point to ask the breeder as many questions as possible about any history of illnesses in the parents, their character, and their behavior.

How to Solve and Deal with Aggression

Aggression in golden retrievers as mentioned earlier can start as early as when they are 6 weeks of age. It is fairly uncommon in golden retrievers but if you have picked up a puppy, which was the most dominant one among the litter, or a puppy that has experienced abuse, or if it has inherited dominance from the parents, it is possible that your puppy may exhibit aggression.

At the age of 6 weeks, a puppy should be socialized with other people and dogs and this period can last until the puppy turns 14 weeks of age or sometimes a little more. Socialization plays an important role to avoid the onset of aggression.

There are a few precautionary measures that will help

avoid aggression in golden retrievers. Do not take away a golden puppy from its litter before it's at least 8 weeks of age. Also, do not use any harsh tactics or behavior with a golden puppy between the ages of 6 to 14 weeks ensuring that it is treated gently during this period. Harsh behavior, yelling or hitting at such a young age can result in your golden turning aggressive over time.

Aggression can be triggered due to various reasons but one of the major factors that will trigger aggression will be the environment in which your golden was. Poor living conditions, insufficient food, cruel owners, strict breeder, etc. are all major factors that can contribute to the build of aggressive behavior in your golden. When you see early signs of aggression, you as an owner can do a few things to control this behavior.

The first step is to determine the reason for the aggression - is it related to an illness or pain, if so, treating it with the help of a veterinarian is a good solution.

Another reason for aggression in golden retrievers could be another dog and its fear, unfamiliar situations, etc. This can mostly be solved by diverting your golden's mind to something else or something that it likes that can be used as an incentive, but make sure that you do not reward it for its aggressive behavior.

So, do not give your golden any treats, but instead teach it to stay or sit while pretending that this is a normal situation and that nothing is wrong. Golden retrievers are smart and when you pretend that the situation is completely normal and do not give it any attention, it will learn that you are not giving any reaction. Then it will stop pursuing such behavior in the future. After a few times of doing this, you will learn that it only takes a look from you to discourage such behavior and make it stop its aggression.

Something that is seldomly discussed is that aggression in all its various forms is not always bad. It is common behavior for an adult golden to growl at a puppy that is new to the environment. It is a way of establishing a relationship and stopping the adult from doing its regular routine that may result in your golden growing even more hostile.

One of the best things about golden retrievers is that they are friendly, intelligent, and they desire for human company and human attention. Thus they are people pleasers because they want their owner or family's attention that they are a part of. It is therefore easy to curtail any aggression in a golden just by training or solving other issues that might have been the origin of the issue.

Strategies and Techniques to Deal with Aggression

You can deploy the following 4 tips that will help control aggression in your golden retriever. A young puppy can be over excited and may lack discipline, but since goldens are intelligent, it is not very difficult to teach it to be obedient and wise. The following principles will help you make the process easier.

Leash Walking

A leash will always help keep your golden in a state of mind that is calm. When your golden is calm, it will respond well and the chances of it getting aggressive will be less too.

A leash will pose a problem only when you allow your golden to run. You have to understand that with a leash in the hand, you are in total control when you take your golden for a walk. If your golden is pulling the leash, then take a break and make it sit down for a while before continuing with the walk.

Obedience

Obedience classes are essential if you have a golden retriever or any other breed for that matter. And obedience classes work for both the dog and the master since it teaches your dog to be balanced and obedient. And as an owner, it will teach you techniques to manage your pet in a better way.

Show leadership and not domination

You need to understand your position as a leader and not a dominating master who may come across as hostile to your golden retriever. By being a leader, your golden will learn to obey you. This means that you need to be a person who is inspiring and trustworthy and not aggressive. In contrast, if you are verbally or physically violent with the golden, it will always associate violence to your relationship.

Consistency

Consistency is the most important thing when it comes to educating your golden retriever. Goldens are very smart and if you wish for your golden to be wise, education by repetition is the key. Constant and habitual methods will train your golden in a disciplined manner. Inform all your family members to be consistent with the methods you use, and it will lead to amazing results.

Is it Common to Find an Aggressive Golden Retriever?

Aggression is not a common characteristic in golden retrievers at all. In fact, goldens are known to be the complete opposite. Unlike other dogs, goldens are also completely fine with having a lower rank or position in the house and are not at all competitive to rise up that ladder. They generally do not have the temperament to be the dominating ones at homes or even with other dogs. So, if a golden does get aggressive, establishing the reason is important.

Different Types of Aggression

Aggression comes in two forms in all dogs and in golden retrievers as well.

1. True Aggression: It is caused because there is not enough release of energy.

2. Reactive Aggression: Caused as a result of an external entity that has annoyed your golden retriever.

Both are equally harmful and can affect your golden and therefore, it is advisable to seek advice from a trainer if it gets too difficult to tackle this on your own.

Ways to Measure Aggression in your Dog

Understanding the cause of aggression is the primary step to know how you can go about fixing it. While a golden commonly is not an aggressive breed, it is still a dog and cannot be exempted from aggressive behavior. In the end, it all depends on the experience your golden has had.

Aggression in goldens could be associated with fear and if that is true, you need to figure the root cause of the fear and why is your golden having this fear of something or someone. There are chances that you have ended up adopting a golden, which had issues or overlooked its past experiences as a puppy. Aggression is often built as a result of reactive behavior to something that your golden is not really fond of.

Possible Causes of Aggression

Two of the most common reason as to why your golden could be aggressive is that:

1. You may lack knowledge about the breed and are not treating it in a way that it prefers to be treated.

2. Separation from previous parents or an old family at a really young age.

It can again be related to the energy that golden retrievers have. Since they have a lot of energy as we have discussed earlier, if this energy is not released properly, your golden may try to figure it out on its own leading to some kind of aggression.

Chapter Ten: Golden Retrievers and Weight Issues

Causes of Weight Gain in Golden Retrievers

Obesity in dogs can have cascading effects on their health as it might not only cause irreversible illnesses but also lower the life expectancy by 2 years. Few of many illnesses that goldens suffer from are heart condition, diabetes, and thyroid problems. A study conducted by the Association for Pet Obesity Prevention (APOP) stated that over 54% of the dogs in the United States are now classified as obese.

As an owner, it is your responsibility to create and stick to the habits that can improve your golden's weight and get them back to being healthy. To be able to do that, it is also important to understand the root cause of the weight gain and work on them to get good results. The following are the reasons that contribute towards obesity in a golden retriever.

Addiction to Treats

Due to its looks and the ability to build a relationship with humans instantly, golden retrievers are susceptible to getting more treats than they are supposed to. It is one thing to reward them for good behavior but another when you go overboard and feed them insistently which can cause weight gain over time.

Even by using tools that helps dispense treats, it can get tricky in some cases as golden retrievers are known for their intelligence, they can adapt and learn the trick of the trade faster than one can imagine. This makes the process of using a machine to dispense treats a failure. Therefore, giving treats by hand is a more suitable option for you as an owner.

Genetic Predisposition

Due to the nature of the golden retriever, they are more likely to get obese. In such scenarios, it is your responsibility as an owner to take measures that ensure good health of the golden. Having bigger homes with yards or timely walks and runs in the park constitutes as physical activity for them as this helps shed any weight, or better yet prevent any type of weight gain in them. In addition to exercise, it is also important for you to feed timely meals, which contain nutrients that can help its recovery and keep them fit for years to come.

Lack of Exercise and Overeating

It is in their nature that dogs foraged for their own food but were not given food by anyone during the earlier times. With evolution, dogs have been tamed and domesticated by their owners, which makes them dependent on their owner for food. Since the change of events calls for different living conditions, golden retrievers, or for that matter any dog, in this process tend to overeat throughout the day.

In addition to their eating habits, due to smaller homes, it also gets harder for golden retrievers to have activity throughout the day. This is the primary reason for obesity in them. The amount of exercise it needs also depends on the age at which it is in.

Age of The Golden

Every breed of dog goes through the cycle of weight gain

through either excessive consumption of food or not exercising at all. One of the ways a golden can gain weight is depending on their age. It is noticed that at every stage, the metabolism of the golden changes, which results in the alteration of the food consumed.

A simple reason for the same is, often times with growing age, their metabolism rate slows down drastically, which means fewer calories burn throughout the day. If it consumes more than it can burn, this additional food turns into fat and gets stored within the body. Therefore, it is important for you as the owner to pay attention to the weight as the older it gets, the higher the chances for them to gain weight.

Pregnancy

If the female golden is not sterilized and goes through a recent heat cycle, chances are it might get in contact with a male dog. If you see your female dog gain weight, it is important for you to contact your vet immediately as it might have gotten pregnant.

Stress

Stress and anxiety can cause weight gain in a golden as it often over consumes food when it is stressed. In humans and dogs alike, stress releases a hormone called cortisol. This hormone is what causes the body to stop burning calories, which implies food converting into fat and resulting in weight gain. It is important for the owner to notice any signs of over-eating and restlessness paired with isolation as signs of them being under stress.

While these are the obvious reasons that can cause weight gain in a golden, the most un-diagnosed reasons for weight gain are the following.

Hypothyroidism

For the body to perform its functions properly, it is important for all the organs and hormones to work in harmony. Sometimes the break-down of one hormone can cause a ripple effect in the health of the dog resulting in weight gain. One of the reasons for weight gain in golden retrievers is when the thyroid gland in its body does not produce enough thyroid hormones thus slowing down the metabolism. This results in less or no calorie burn during the process for food consumption and leads to weight gain.

Feeding the Wrong Food

The nutritional requirement for a puppy versus an adult golden is very different. In every stage the portion of carbs/fats/proteins changes, therefore, it is important to keep an eye on what food you give it. This is also based on the activity level of the golden at every stage. While it is justified to consume higher amounts of protein and carbohydrates when it is a puppy, we cannot say the same for when it is growing older. Therefore, feeding the wrong food at the wrong stage of its life can result in serious weight gain and this leads to some irreversible damage to its body.

Water Retention and Bloating

An endocrine disorder, which is also known as the Cushing disease, is caused when the golden has an increased level of cortisol in its body. This results in a high amount of water retention, which in turn causes bloating. In Cushing disease, the golden often loses its muscle mass and starts to exhibit skin problems and urinates excessively.

Few other reasons that can cause bloating in them are heart diseases and cancer. For example, due to heart disease, it gets harder for blood to get pumped effectively throughout the body causing fluid to leak through the vessels into the abdomen or the chest. This makes the golden look bloated from the belly or the chest. In such scenarios, it is important to consult a vet immediately and get the right treatment.

Prescription Drugs

You probably know that every drug ever prescribed by

the vet has some side effects that are not obvious but sometimes show up. In one scenario, a drug called Prednisone often mimics Cushing disease when given in high dosages for a longer period of time. This causes bloating and weight gain. In such cases consult your vet and switch to a different drug or a different approach to the problem. Be sure to keep an eye on its diet as well.

Health Problems Associated to Weight Gain

Though weight gain may look like a problem in itself, it is important for you as the owner to know that weight gain can be a symptom leading to a bigger problem. Most of the weight gain is reversible when action is taken on time. If neglected, it can lead to some serious cases of illnesses such as:

- High blood pressure
- Internal organ damage, particularly liver and kidneys.
- Arthritis
- Diabetes
- Various Forms of Cancer
- Digestive Issues
- Increased risk of infection due to their immune system being compromised.
- Damage to bones, joints, and soft tissues.
- Respiratory Diseases
- Heart Diseases.
- Heat Intolerance

These problems do not just stop there. With weight gain, the golden puts a lot of pressure on its joints causing sores and calluses on their hocks and elbows as they tend to lay down for longer periods of time. Apart from this, they also are prone to suffer from hip and elbow dysplasia, which are developmental abnormalities in the joints that can lead to pain in those areas. This problem tends to get worsened due to that extra weight being carried by them causing a lifetime of discomfort.

Diet and Nutrition for a Healthy Golden Retriever

It can be unnerving to find yourself trying to figure out a feeding schedule with the right nutrient content that goes into the food for your golden puppy. To ensure that you are providing the right food in the right proportions, it is important to maintain a feeding chart with the time schedule attached to it. At every stage of the dog feeding schedule, the number of meals and what to feed your dog changes. Therefore, it is important to visit the vet and make alterations to the food based on its requirements.

The ideal weights for a golden retriever based on its gender are:

- For males, it is between 65 - 75 lbs.
- For females, it is between 55 - 75 lbs.

Before you can start feeding your golden with food, it is important to know the current weight of the puppy. You can know this by feeling the ribs of your golden. As it covered by natural coating, it can be hard to locate its ribs visually. Therefore, feeling the ribs by placing your hand on their ribs can be one of the ways to know if your golden is underweight or overweight. If you are able to feel the ribs slightly and they are not visibly seen from outside, then your golden is in its ideal weight. If you find it hard to feel the ribs, then it is an indication that your puppy is overweight or obese.

At two months old, your golden puppy might need to be fed two or more times a day. They usually consume half a cup of food a meal making it 1.5 cups of food every day. This changes when the golden puppy is three months old where it can eat up to 2 cups of food in a day split into three servings. At five to six months, this increases to 3 to 3.5 cups of food split in three servings. Post this, the average amount of food a golden can have is 4 cups split into equal portions per meal in a day depending on the size, gender, and age.

As there are two food types that can be fed to a golden, mainly dry and wet foods, it is important to have a smooth transition when you are changing the food from what the breeder has given to you to what is needed for the dog of its age. Therefore, it is important to consult a vet and take their recommendations of food groups to be added to your dog's meals.

For a growing pup, in dry foods, you can choose brands that specify that they are rich in Omega-3 and Omega-6 fatty acids, protein for bone and muscle building, L-carnitine for muscle and joint development, and antioxidants. Micro-doses of vitamins and minerals is also recommended.

As golden retrievers are quick learners, getting them used to different textures and tastes of food can also help you to transition or switch foods whenever necessary. The choice of giving wet food to your golden is more individual. You can give your golden dry food as well as wet food as a treat or use it as a substitute for hydration if you see them not drinking water frequently. Both dry and wet foods have various choices of meat you can choose from such as lamb, chicken, beef, and turkey.

If you have a golden puppy that is allergic to certain types of foods or has a sensitive stomach, take your time in noticing which of the foods given to them triggered such conditions. Puppies with allergies are often recommended a diet that focuses on eliminating any type of artificial food preservatives and enhancers. It is recommended to choose foods such as chicken, fish, and eggs as sources of protein and to eat lots of fruits and vegetables, instead of adding these artificial food preservatives and enhancers.

You can be feeding your golden puppy the right way but be cautious about overfeeding them as this may result in a condition called "Panosteitis", also known as the "growing pains". This is a condition where they tend to put on maximum weight while transitioning. This can result in exerting high pressure on the joints leading to hip and joint illness later in their life.

Overfeeding can also occur while giving your puppies treats for good behavior. The amount of treats can be controlled by reducing the frequency at which you give them treats and by choosing an alternative way to reward them. You can also make healthier treats with wholesome ingredients at home thus eliminating the artificially flavored treats.

Best Types of Exercises for Golden Retrievers

Known for their energy and fitness levels, for a long time, the primary reason for breeding golden retrievers were to make them good hunters. As time passed by, they have now learned to fit into families as their companions. Provided with large space and numerous amounts of activities it can get in a day, golden retrievers can be promising companions in your fitness journey. The following are few of the many activities you can plan together or plan for your golden.

Walking or Running

You will be surprised to see the ability of your golden to keep up with you on your fitness journey. Starting off with a simple walk a day, they can walk for more than an hour as they are known to be athletic. If you plan to go out for a run, they can accompany you with ease as they can keep up with your running pace and not get tired.

Fetch

If you want to keep your golden excited and active, playing fetch is one of the easiest options. Since they love to play fetch, taking them to a park and playing with them is a great form of exercise. Keep in mind that they will need timely breaks if they are getting back to fitness after a long time of not exercising.

A large amount of extensive exercising might put pressure on their joints, which can damage them and cause lots of problems over time. For playing fetch, understand whether they get distracted easily. If yes, then choose a closed yard where they can concentrate on you. Also, ensure to choose soft toys over heavy and sharp objects while playing.

Dock Diving and Swimming

Golden retrievers love water so naturally, it loves to swim. They are known to be natural swimmers. Therefore, swimming or dock diving can be a great way to get them up and running. Due to their natural protective coating, they are resistant to cold weather and can easily dry themselves. If you plan to take your golden to the beach or to the swimming pool, ensure to free them of their collars or any apparel before they dive in and watch them while they swim.

Although they are natural swimmers, accidents can happen, especially their collars getting snagged in the pool. If you want to be extra careful, you can suit them up in their swimming vest and let them go crazy. Make sure to give them a good bath after their swim to get rid of any dirt or chlorine and dry them off after. It is also important to clean their ears to avoid any ear infections.

Hide and Seek

If you are concerned about giving your golden too many treats, you can hide yourself instead of hiding treats and let it search for you. You can distract it with its favorite toy and as it starts playing with the toy, you can hide yourself. If it immediately doesn't try to find you, you can tell it to come to you using the "come" command, thereby reinforcing the training. This is a great form of exercise as it distracts the golden from eating too many treats while getting its share of exercising too.

Agility Training

Golden retrievers love it when they are completely occupied by mind and body. One way to achieve that is through dog agility training. You can find an agility group nearby or set up your own in your backyard with the help of some hula hoops, tables, things to balance on your golden, or things that your golden can balance on. This form of training also builds a great and meaningful bond between you and your golden as it allows you two to work for a common goal.

Jumping

Jumping is a fun activity that can get you and your golden both on your feet. Jumping is a great exercise for both you and your dog and it burns a lot of calories. Try grabbing its favorite toy and squat down and make some noises with it so that it knows you have the toy and let it jump up to get its toy back from you. Something more fun is to blow non-toxic bubbles in the air and let it chase it and pop them. You can find non-toxic peanut butter flavored bubbles that are easily digestible by golden retrievers.

Frequency of Exercises

While it is hard to summarize into one paragraph as to how much exercise is good exercise for a golden retriever, goldens have the ability to keep up and stay focused on playing for long hours. It is important to keep your golden's age, size, and health in mind and consult the vet to understand the hours of exercise activity it needs. For a puppy, an activity of 5 minutes a day per each month in age is important as it needs to be fed and sleep for the maximum part of the day.

Once the puppy turns 3 months old, activity of 15 minutes per day is recommended and once it turns 5 months old, activity of 25 minutes is sufficient for it to stay fit. For an average grown golden, a good one hour of exercise of your choice can help it to stay fit and active. The more energetic your golden is, it will need a larger amount of daily exercise.

Since there is no hard and fast rule of exercising, it is up to you on what kind of exercises you would like to choose for it. It is a great opportunity for you and your golden to bond as they tend to feel happier when they are active. If you notice that your golden is not paying enough attention to you, chewing your belongings, or seeming generally out of control, then that serves as an indication for you that it is not getting enough exercise each day. So, take them out on a run or a walk and choose agility training to keep them occupied as this will help them become more relaxed.

****

Before you go on to the next chapter....

If you find this information beneficial to you, we would really appreciate your thoughts on the book.

Please feel free to take a minute and write an honest review !
Reviews from awesome readers like you are important for our books.

****

Chapter Eleven: Cancer in Golden Retrievers

Are you aware of the fact that your golden retriever is susceptible to cancer just like any other human being? There are certain breeds of dogs that are prone to cancer, and unfortunately your golden retriever falls in this category. So, it is important for you to learn more about cancer in golden retrievers and how to prevent or treat it.

How Common is Cancer in Golden Retrievers?

Around the late 1980s, cancer was not really a major concern for golden retrievers. The rate of cancer in this breed actually shot up around the late 1990s when there was a sudden spike in cancer amongst the golden retrievers in the U.S. Research also says that dogs in the U.S. are at higher risk than those in European countries. There are studies being conducted to look into this and identify the risk factors.

How to Prevent Cancer?

Like any other disease, there are always precautions that will help to prevent the disease in the first place, even though they aren't "full proof". You can take some steps to help protect your retriever from the risk of cancer.

Control Weight Gain

Firstly, you must prevent excessive weight gain in your golden retriever. It can be tempting to feed them every time they look at you with those puppy eyes but being overweight increases their risk of cancer. There is a lot of research being conducted on this, and a lot of it shows that reducing the number of calories in the dog's diet can help to prevent or delay the development of tumors. The growth of any cancerous tumor will be blocked if the body is given fewer calories.

On the other hand, excess calories will cause obesity, which in turn can increase the risk of cancer. The factors that are usually at work in obesity have also shown to have an impact on cancer. This includes insulin sensitivity and oxidative stress. So, keep your dog healthy and running in order to avoid excess fat deposition in its body.

Control Inflammation

Inflammation in the body increases the risk of cancer. This is why you need to focus on finding a diet that is anti-inflammatory for your golden retriever. Carbohydrates fuel inflammation in the body and this considerably increases the risk of cancer. Abnormal cancer cells tend to proliferate in the environment created by inflammation. The cancer cells themselves require energy for growth and cutting down on glucose will help to reduce their growth rate.

Some foods that you need to restrict are fructose-laden fruits, processed grains, and potatoes or other starchy vegetables. Even the dry pet food you give your dog will usually contain a certain amount of starch. Increase the amount of dietary fat from healthy sources instead of carbohydrates. This is because these fats are usually not used for energy by cancerous cells, unlike glucose. Reduce the amount of protein, increase fats, and try to reduce carbohydrates.

Inflammation in the body is also noticed if the retriever's diet contains insufficient omega 3's and excessive omega 6 fatty acids, which causes an unhealthy imbalance. This is how the processed pet foods you buy at the store are loaded. You need to reverse this since the latter increases inflammation while the former reduces it. Try to switch over from this and feed your dog a wholesome diet.

In the same way natural foods are better for humans, they can also benefit a dog's health. Find high-quality sources of protein like bones, organs, and meat, along with animal fat and some servings of fresh vegetables with a low glycemic index value. The moisture content in this kind of diet will be high without any starchy or grainy food. You can also try adding some probiotics, digestive enzymes, and green foods to enhance the immune function of your dog.

Eliminate Exposure to Toxins

Find a way to either completely get rid of toxins in the environment or reduce them for the sake of your dog's health. Toxins increase the risk of cancer in your dog, and you need to reduce exposure as much as you can, even though the modern world is full of it. Start by keeping certain items out of their reach, such as flame-retardants, lawn chemicals (like weed killers), and flea or tick preventives.

Household cleaners like detergents, soaps, and dryer sheets should also be kept away. Try to find the most dog-friendly products possible or try making your own formulas that are less toxic and have more organic components. It is not possible to completely protect them from exposure to toxins, so try to get a detoxification guide from the vet.

Right Vaccination

Don't let your golden retriever get every single vaccination in the market just because they market the vaccines for the health of your dog. The protocol for vaccines should be to maximize the protection of your dog and reduce the risk. Try to avoid the combination of vaccines that a lot of veterinary practices recommend. It is immunologically-risky and not necessary at all.

Instead, try to give them a single Parvo vaccine followed by a distemper vaccine when they are 12 weeks old. The second set can be given at 14 weeks. After this, we recommend a laboratory blood test two weeks after the previous one. The dog should be immunized successfully by then and will be protected all through their life.

All of these above steps can help to prevent cancer in your beloved golden retriever and can protect them throughout their life.

What Age Do Golden Retrievers Get Cancer?

Nearly half of these dogs are diagnosed with cancer after they reach the age of 10. The rate of mortality is higher depending on how much bigger the dog is. This is why small dogs, like Chihuahuas, have about a 10% risk while golden retrievers have anywhere up to 60%. Male golden retrievers are even more prone to cancer than females.

Signs of Cancer in Golden Retrievers

You should look out for the following signs and symptoms that might arise if your golden retriever gets cancer. It is terrible to contemplate your dog getting this unforgiving disease, but you still need to be wary of it.

1) **Lumps and Masses**
   A lump or mass might grow. If there is any such growth in your dog, especially around their paws or legs, then take them to the vet. The dark growths are usually signs of melanoma, and you need to be wary if the growth appears to increase in size over time.

2) **Foul Breath**
   Look out for unusually foul breath. You might think that dogs always have bad breath, but with oral cancer the odor can be particularly foul. Groom your retriever's mouth regularly so that you can tell if the smell seems unusually different and bad.

3) **Abnormal Discharge**

    Another symptom is abnormal discharge. If you notice any unusual fluid discharge, like pus or blood, then you should immediately notify the vet. In the case of cancerous cells in the GI tract, there is excessive secretion of such fluids.

4) **Bloating**

    Bloating in your dog can also be worrisome. If there is a tumor growing in the GI tract, then fluids may build up and cause a swollen belly. So, look out for any abnormal bloating.

5) **Excessive Weight Loss**

    Although we said that excessive weight gain is the main concern, you also need to look out for excessive weight loss. If your retriever loses too much weight suddenly, then it might be a symptom of lymphoma. They tend to lose weight and get very tired when ridden with this type of cancer.

6) **Signs of Lethargy**

    You also have to look out for any signs of lethargy. Has your normally-active dog been acting lazy? See if they are reluctant to go for a walk or play with their toy. If this behavior continues, then it can indicate cancer or other diseases.

7) **Difficulties and Discomfort While Eating**
Oral cancer will make it difficult for your retriever to eat. Look out for any signs of discomfort while swallowing because that can be a sign.

8) **Changes in Bathroom Habits**
Cancer in the kidneys or bladder will cause changes in your dog's bathroom habits. Pay attention when they are relieving themselves and notice if they have any trouble urinating. They might even have difficulty with bowel movements. Such discomfort will also make your dog reluctant to relieve themselves.

9) **Nausea**
Another symptom of certain types of cancer is nausea. If your dog is afflicted, they will have a sudden loss of appetite. It is easy to spot this symptom since golden retrievers tend to be hungry all the time when they are healthy. So, if it looks like they aren't eating their food or they ignore their treats, then you need to check with the vet.

10) **Growths and Bumps**
Any type of cancer can result in the growth of bumps or wounds on the skin of your dog. These don't heal and tend to look abnormal, so you should keep an eye out for them. Do a regular

check of your dog's skin to make sure no unusual growths appear.

11) Difficulty in Breathing

They can also suffer from difficulty in breathing due to cancers in their heart or lungs. Tumors in these regions usually cause irregular respiration.

12) Difficulty in Urination

Just like we said, you should notice any difficulty in urination, but you also ought to see if they urinate too frequently. If there is a tumor growing in the hypothalamus, then they will feel excessively thirsty and drink a lot of water. This will result in increased urination, which is a symptom of cancer as well.

All of these symptoms need to be kept in mind. You should check your golden retriever for any signs on a regular basis. Pay attention to their behavior, and if you notice any unusual change, then let a veterinarian know. The faster you catch symptom the earlier you can help your dog.

Common Reason for Death in Golden Retrievers

It is always better to be prepared than caught unaware. It

may be hard to think of your golden retriever dying, but they will at some point. In order to ensure a long and healthy life, you have to know the various causes of death in this breed. This will help you take the right precautions and prevent as many diseases as possible.

The biggest cause of fatality in this breed is cancer. Nearly 61% of golden retrievers die from cancer, according to research. The common types of cancer are: lymphosarcoma (cancer of the lymphoid tissues and lymphocytes, which is a type of blood cell) osteosarcoma (cancer that causes weak bones), and hemangiosarcoma (fast growing cancer that affects the walls of blood vessels). Before a puppy is sold or given for adoption, reputable breeders try to screen them for any such diseases.

Hip and Elbow Dysplsia: Hip and elbow dysplasia are found in at least one-fifth of the retrievers.

Eye Diseases such as cataract, might also afflict golden retrievers. Some other ailments related to the eye include entropic now, retinal dysplasia, glaucoma, and corneal dystrophy.

Heart Diseases: You also need to look out for heart diseases that can be fatal for this breed. Cardiomyopathy and subvalvular aortic stenosis are the usual heart conditions that tend to afflict golden retrievers.

Joint Diseases may also occur. These include osteochondritis, ligament rupture, and patella luxation.

Some other illnesses that you need to look out for are hemophilia, lick granuloma, and seborrhea.

All of these are the most common diseases that have been found to affect the health of golden retrievers, but cancer is the most common killer that you need to protect them from.

Chapter Twelve: Golden Retrievers and Water

As mentioned earlier, a golden retriever is recognized easily because of their cheerful temperament and their gorgeous coat. They are playful, well-mannered, and obedient. Unlike most dogs, a golden retriever loves the water and endlessly craves outdoor activities. Do you know why that is? This chapter will help you understand more about why a golden loves the water as much as it does.

Behavior Characteristics That Cause Them to Love Water

A golden retriever, as discussed earlier, was bred for the job of retrieving the game, especially ducks, for a hunter. This breed is originally from Scotland and was used to find prey and retrieve it after the prey was shot. There were many situations where the golden had to step into a body of water to retrieve the prey. Since the retriever has a dense outer coat that repels water and a thick undercoat that protects it from the cold, it can jump into water and swim for hours. These characteristics make it easier for a retriever to swim with its parent.

Some experts suggest that a retriever loves the water because of the initial breeding process where a water spaniel was crossed with a yellow flat-coated retriever. The offspring of this cross were allowed to mate with water spaniels and other breeds. Genetics, however, do not always play a major role. This is because there are some retrievers that prefer to stay away from water.

Most golden retrievers love the water, but there are some who do not want to wet their coat. There are numerous puppies who hate swimming. They will, however, love to go into the water when they grow up. This has more to do with their environment and their upbringing.

If the pup's mother is careful and introduces the pup to water carefully, then the pup will enjoy swimming. It will continue to enjoy it as it grows up. Since it easy to train a golden retriever, it will be extremely easy for you to train it to swim. Swimming is a good source of exercise, and it is important for your golden's overall wellbeing and mental stimulation.

Danger in Water

It is unfortunate that swimming does come with some issues. Goldens who are adept at swimming sometimes will find themselves in trouble. Therefore, as a parent, it is important that you always keep the following points in mind when your golden is in the water.

Never Assume that Your Dog Will Love Water

It is important to remember that not every golden is the same. There are some goldens who are anxious or afraid of water. If your golden has such a fear, then ensure that you do not force it into the water. You should also know that your golden does not necessarily need to have fun in the water just because it used to enjoy swimming in the past.

Always Remain by Your Dog's Side

A golden is known to love the water, and as mentioned

earlier it loves to play in the water. This does not mean that you leave it alone in the water. Ensure that you are close to your golden when it is in the water. You can also buy your golden a dog life jacket. This way your dog can relax in the water and float.

Introduce Your Dog to Swimming

If your golden is new to swimming, it is important to remember to go slow. You should first introduce it to the idea of swimming and be patient. You should snap the life jacket on and use your golden's favorite toy as a motivator.

Toss the toy into the shallow end of the water, then let your golden splash and fetch the joy. Praise it when it retrieves the toy. Ensure that you pay attention to your dog's behavior and responses. If your dog shows anxiety or fear, then stop the session immediately. You can always continue the activity on the following day.

Teach Your Golden to Get Out of Water

There are many parents who know that their golden will have fun in the water, but they forget to teach it how to get out of the water. It is important to teach your pups how to do this, especially if there is no natural shore to the body of water. You should always teach your golden to come back to an exit point. Ensure that you find a spot around the water body that is safe for your dog. Call it to that exit point when you want it to step out of the water.

Keep the Leash On

When you are teaching your pup to swim, you must always keep it on a leash. This will help you pull it back if there is an emergency. It is always a good idea if you can enter the water with your golden. You should only take the leash off your golden once you are certain that it can swim without your assistance and that it always comes to you when you call.

Ensure That They are Safe from Other Dangerous Animals

If you swim with your dog in a lake, river, or when traveling in a boat, then you should remember that any wild animal can be dangerous. Alligator, sharks, snakes, and other animals may look at your golden and attack it. This is because it looks like a delicious snack. This is an issue in some parts of the U.S., but moose, coyotes, and bears can also be dangerous.

You should never take your dog for a swim in a lake or river if you are unsure of its skills. You should always carry bear spray (used as a deterrant to aggressive bears) with you if you want to ward off the most dangerous threats, even for just a short period.

Always Be Cautious in Unfamiliar Water Bodies

Unfamiliar bodies of water will hold many hazards that can affect your golden. Some risks include unknown water depths, high levels of bacteria and other microorganisms, stinging jellyfish, parasites, broken glass, rip tides, and undertow. You should always be smart and check the water body before you go for a swim with your golden. If you are unsure of the body of water, then avoid going there. You should conduct thorough research before you take a dip in that body of water.

Always Be Vigilant When You Sail

You must remember that your golden will panic when you are on a boat and the water is choppy. You should ensure that you keep your golden confined to its leash or at least wearing a life jacket. You should ensure that your dog is always in your eyesight, and if it falls overboard, then ensure that you guide it to a safe spot that is close to you so that you can then rescue it. Since your dog can fall off the boat or swim away from you, it is important that you never allow your golden to swim alone. Either you or another friend should swim with it.

Activities to Do with Your Golden in the Water

It is easy to train a golden retriever. It is because of this that it is easy for you to teach it how to swim. If you have a golden retriever at home and you love to swim, then you will never find a better companion. A golden retriever will not only love to play fetch in a pond or pool but will also love to accompany you to your favorite beach or lakeside retreat. It is always good to allow your golden to swim since it is the best form of exercise for it. It is also a good way to ensure that it is tired and will sleep well throughout the night.

When your golden is a pup, you should introduce it to water. Allow it to explore everything about water by itself. If your pup is wary of its surroundings, then you can swim with it in the water to encourage it. You should, however, let it take its own time to adjust to the water.

If you want to motivate your golden, then you can throw its favorite toy in the water. If it does not retrieve the toy, then you should go ahead and retrieve it yourself. As mentioned earlier, you should be careful when it comes to taking your golden on a boat ride.

Water Retrieving

A golden retriever loves to play fetch and retrieves any object that you want it to bring. This is one of the only dog breeds that can fetch any object, and they love to look for toys. It also enjoys carrying objects in its mouth. Swimming is a great way to give your golden some aerobic exercise.

You can also purchase a water toy, which floats. Throw this toy around and play fetch with your golden. You should first practice this activity on land, then ensure that you find a safe space in the water where you can play fetch with your golden. As mentioned earlier, there are many risks associated with outdoor swimming, like pollution, cold weather, obstructions, and currents. You should also ensure that your golden can get out of the water safely if you allow it to swim alone.

Swimming

Swimming is one of the best activities that you can perform with your golden retriever. This exercise will help both you and your golden to stay cool during summer. As mentioned earlier, a golden retriever is a natural swimmer. This is because of its special coat, which protects it from feeling too cold. It also dries off quickly. If you do not own a private pool, then you can always swim with your golden in the lake if the lake is dog-friendly. It is also a good idea to invest in a small pool at home.

When you swim with your golden, you must ensure that it is not wearing its collar or other apparel, besides a life jacket. You should always keep an eye on your golden to ensure that it is safe. It is true that a golden is a natural swimmer, but accidents can happen. Its collar might get snagged. It is always good to put on a dog life vest. You should always take it slow when you are swimming with your puppy.

How to Care for Your Golden After a Swim?

You should always shower your golden with praises and treats if you are teaching it to swim. When you finish the training session, ensure that you bathe your golden well after the swim to get rid of the dirt, chlorine, and any other substances that can cause infections. It will also feel good for your dog. You must ensure that your dog is safe.

Observe your dog for a few days after the swim. This is because any infection caused by bacteria or other parasites will not become obvious immediately after a swim. You should observe your dog, and if you notice any unusual behavior or symptoms, then take it immediately to the vet.

****
Before you keep on reading…..

Finding this book helpful? Take a breather and leave an honest review.

Reviews are super important for our books and we would really appreciate your thoughts!

****

Chapter Thirteen: Incontinence Issues

Golden Retrievers and Incontinence

If your potty-trained golden retriever starts losing control of their bladder and starts leaking urine everywhere, most likely they are experiencing urinary incontinence. Despite being potty-trained, your golden can start losing control of their own bladder and leak urine in different places around your home. There can be many reasons why these symptoms occur, so it is important that you consult with your vet if you see your golden show signs of urinary incontinence.

Causes for Urinary Incontinence

Golden Retrievers are one of the breeds at high-risk for urinary incontinence. Some of the other breeds in this list also include Labrador retrievers and Siberian huskies just to name a few. As for the causes of urinary incontinence, there are several of them.

Some causes of incontinence are:

- Urinary tract infection
- Hormonal imbalance
- Bladder stones
- Weak urethral sphincter

- Spinal degeneration or injury

- Prostate disorders

- Anatomic disorders

- Diseases like kidney disease, diabetes, and hyperadrenocorticism that lead to excessive consumption of water

- Protruding intervertebral disc

- Medication

- Congenital abnormalities

How to Deal with Incontinence?

It is important to understand the underlying cause for incontinence before you begin treating your golden. Different medicines can be administered to your golden to manage and prevent this condition. There are some treatments that only focus on your golden's hormones, while there are others that will control the flow of urine by strengthening the urethral sphincter.

If the external or internal medication does not work, then you can always look at surgery. A new therapy to treat incontinence has shown some promising results.

You should consider surgery if your golden has developed incontinence because of congenital abnormality, bladder stones, or a protruding disk.

How to Manage Urinary Incontinence?

- Pile a few clean towels and blankets in your golden's favorite spot. You can also use some rubber sheets or waterproof pads. These will absorb a lot of the moisture.

- You should take your golden for a walk every morning and when it wakes up from a nap. Ensure that you take it for a lot of walks.

- Use a dog diaper if you are unable to control the situation. These diapers can be found online or at most pet stores.

- Always check with the vet before you reduce your golden's water intake.

- Ensure that you take your golden to the vet if you see it develop any skin infections.

- It is always important to monitor your dog's condition, especially when it comes to older dogs since they develop infections quickly.

Dog Diapers

You can use a dog diaper if your golden displays incontinence. There is a debate about what diaper you should use for your golden. You can choose between a cloth and disposable diaper. You can be environmentally-conscious when you use a cloth diaper. This is because you can wash it and reuse it on your golden.

That being said, you will constantly need to wash the diapers to ensure that there are fresh ones for your dog. The initial cost of owning cloth diapers is higher than a disposable diaper. On the other hand, it is easy to use a disposable diaper since you will get rid of it.

There are different types of dog diapers that are available on the market. There are some owners who like to use a belly band diaper for their male dogs. This diaper has a shell that is placed on your dog's midsection. They can also buy full diapers, which are the size of a diaper for babies. You can also make a diaper for your golden if you want.

How to Use Dog Diapers?

You should follow the instructions on the product.

There are different diapers to cater to variations in absorbency and fit. The instructions will help you choose the right product for your dog.

Your dog is like a baby, which means that you should change the diaper as often as you can. If you leave a soiled or wet diaper on for too long, then your golden can develop a rash, which can lead to itching, burning, inflammation, and other bacterial infections.

Always use baby wipes when you change your dog's diaper. And try to avoid coming in contact with urine or feces. It is always recommended to wear gloves.

Dog diapers come with a hole for your dog's tail. If your dog does not have a tail or the tail is docked, then you should cover the hole in the diaper. This will help to prevent any leakage.

Remember, you should always consult with the vet before you begin to use dog diapers. There are many reasons for incontinence, and there are other ways to treat this illness.

Pros and Cons

Dog diapers are not only used for dog incontinence, but are also used for:

- Female dogs on their period or menstruation cycle

- Female dogs if you want to avoid mating

- When you travel with your dog

- When you potty train your dog

Chapter Fourteen: Ways to Mentally Stimulate Your Golden Retriever

Benefits of Mental Stimulation and How Does It Affect Your Dog's Brain?

Every dog will need to exercise regularly and maintain a healthy weight to ensure that it is healthy. There are some owners who forget that their dogs also need to be stimulated mentally through some activities. There are many studies that have been conducted over the decade that show that mental stimulation is important for a dog regardless of how old it is.

Experts agree that there is a strong correlation between severe mental illnesses, like anxiety and depression, and the lack of mental stimulation in a dog. This section covers some reasons why it is important to stimulate your dog's mind.

Alleviates Boredom

If you are a parent who is often away from home during the day, then you should remember that your dog might go through separation anxiety. This will lead to some behavioral problems. Your dog displays this behavior because it misses you.

That being said, your dog will bark excessively and tear up your house because it is bored. A bored dog will find a way to entertain itself. To ensure that your dog does not develop destructive habits, you should always leave it with some food puzzles and other activities that will keep it busy throughout the day, thereby alleviating boredom.

Important for Happiness

Mental stimulation also ensures that your dog does not become depressed. Mentally-stimulating activities will keep your dog happy. As a parent of a golden retriever, you need to identify different activities that will keep it entertained and happy.

Lowers Aggression

If you perform the right activities to stimulate your golden's mind, then you can lower its tendency to become aggressive. A bored dog is a cranky dog, and a cranky dog will become aggressive towards other animals and people. It is important to ensure that you perform the right activities to keep your dog mentally stimulated. This is essential if you have kids or other pets at home.

Lowers Stress

Stress can lead to a lot of health issues in both human beings and dogs. If a dog does not receive enough mental stimulation, then it can suffer from some stress, which can lead to depression and anxiety. This can also lead to some issues with behavior and other physical issues.

Gets Rid of Destructive Behavior

A dog who is not mentally stimulated will destroy things, bark incessantly, chew furniture, and display other destructive behavior. PETA reported that many dogs are being re-homed because they display destructive behavior. If the parents provided the right activities for the dog, then it is likely that it would not display such behaviors.

Keeps Older Dogs Mentally Healthy

It is necessary to mentally stimulate older dogs to ensure that their brain activity does not deteriorate. An older dog's mental health is dependent on the different activities that are conducted while it is growing up. It is important to ensure that you do not neglect these activities during the last years. You should use socialization and puzzle toys to stimulate older dogs.

Teaches Young Puppies Good Habits

Socializing, playtime, and mentally-stimulating toys and games are crucial for the development of a puppy. Studies show that these toys and games will make the puppy more confident. They also teach the puppy how to behave properly. It also helps to give the puppy an outlet for extra energy. Puppies will learn how to refrain from displaying destructive behavior and will develop healthy habits.

Helps Bond with Your Dog

Command training, taking your dog for a walk to the park, working on agility training, solving puzzle games, and playing fetch will also improve the bond you share with your dog. There are many owners who have said that a strong bond will ensure that your dog does not misbehave or act out. You can always turn any activity into a game and ensure that your dog is mentally stimulated.

Different Activities and Games

Brain Toys

It is always a good idea to leave your dog with some challenging toys if you want to prevent them from being bored. There are many new dog toys for mental stimulation that are on the market. There are some puzzles that will dispense treats when your dog learns to unlock the mechanism of the puzzle. Examples of some of these toys include:

- Outward Hound Tornado Treat Dispenser
- Dog Twister
- Our Pets IQ Ball

You can give your dog these toys if you do not want to give it food in a bowl. The food that these toys dispense will be the same quantity as your dog's daily breakfast. It will take your golden at least fifteen minutes to obtain its breakfast. When you give your golden these toys to play with when you are not around, it will remain entertained and preoccupied, and it will not miss you when you are away.

Activities

As mentioned earlier, it is important to always challenge your dog's brain to ensure that it stays sharp. Regardless of how old a dog is, it will benefit from the different brain toys and games.

In the previous section, we covered some games and toys that will help to stimulate your golden's brain. When you stimulate your golden's brain, you can ensure that it will socialize with other people and dogs. Your golden will also grow up to be healthy and happy. Thankfully, it is simple to do this since you will only need to play games with your golden.

Hide and Seek

Games that stimulate your dog's mind are not only good for its health but are also a great way to nurture your dog. You can also work on the bond that you share with it. A dog is brilliant and loyal, and it will do anything you ask it to because it loves you. Therefore, all you need to do is take the effort to challenge your dog and play games, like hide and seek.

Pick up your dog's favorite toy and hide it. Ask your dog to go and look for the toy. You must remember to praise your dog, even if it does not find the toy. If you see that it is walking in the right direction, then you must praise it. You can always make the game more interesting by hiding the toy in tricky places. A dog loves a challenge!

Teach the Golden New Words

A dog can not only understand the tone of your voice but also understand words. Therefore, you should teach your golden to perform different activities apart from fetching. You should teach it words and colors. This will help you stimulate their mind.

If your dog has toys in different colors, then you can teach your dog to differentiate between a red toy and a green toy. All you need to do is be patient. Teach your dog to find a green or red toy. When you use positive reinforcement, it will learn faster and understand the difference between the words. If it does find the wrong toy, then you should take the toy from your dog and continue to give it the same instructions. Remember that your dog will need your help in the beginning, but it will soon understand what you are saying.

Find the Treat

You can hide a treat inside some toys (some examples have been given above), and your dog must use his brain to solve the puzzle and retrieve its treat. You can build your own games to stimulate and challenge your dog. This will help it become a happy and well-behaved pet.

Always Use Positive Reinforcement

Remember to be patient when you are training your dog. Even if it does not understand what you are saying, that is okay. You should never shout at them if they make a mistake while trying to understand your command. All you need to do is show it the right direction. When your dog finally brings you the right toy, praise it and give it a treat. Remember to only give it one treat. You only need to let it know that it is doing the right thing.

Toys and Treats for Dogs

There are many colorful toys available in the market (some have been listed above). While using these toys to play games, you'll need treats to reward them and reinforce good behavior. As mentioned earlier, it is always good to use natural treats. Walk into any pet store and pick up some treats whenever you can to ensure no good deed goes unrewarded.

Brain Games

This section has some of the best suggestions for games that you can use to entertain your dog. Mind games or training games for your dog can include anything that will keep it active. You can use clicker training to teach your dog some tricks. This will help you communicate with your dog and also help your dog learn.

There are other games that are available on the internet that you can use to train your dog. One such game, called Four Paws in a Box, is a fun game that you can play with your golden during training. In this game, you will need to teach your dog how to climb into a cardboard box. You can find detailed instructions about how to play the game on the box itself.

It is also a good idea to play nose games with your dog

since it will learn to sniff better. You can add different scents around your house, in your dog's home, and in your yard. It is always a good idea to use safe scents, especially those that are prepared for a dog. These scents can be found online. You can add a scent to the ball you use to play fetch with.

The Long-Term Benefits of Mental Stimulation

As mentioned in the first section of this chapter, it is important to stimulate your golden's mind to reduce boredom. A dog that is mentally active will never develop separation anxiety since it knows how to keep itself busy. This is because it knows how to use the different toys and games to entertain itself. When your dog is mentally stimulated, it will not develop stress or anxiety, and it will be a happy animal.

****

Before we wrap up reading this book, I do have one favor to ask of you. **Please take a minute and write an honest review.**

Reviews are very important for our books and we would really appreciate your thoughts on it!
****

Thank you very much! Please continue reading onto the next page.

Conclusion

As you come to the end of this book, we would like to thank you for downloading it and taking your time to read through all the information.

I hope you found it a good read and informative enough to serve your purpose. Golden retrievers are lovable dogs with a big heart. You just need a little time to train them initially.

This book has enough information to help you understand the different ways your dog might behave in certain situations. You are now equipped to deal with it well. There are many reference books out there that might confuse you with their technical jargon, but this guide is all you really need.

A golden retriever has a simple mind and you can connect with them very easily. Remember to be firm but kind to them no matter what and they will always return ten times the love back to you. Once you get familiar with your golden retriever, you will definitely be telling everyone to adopt one. Don't forget to recommend this book to your friends and family as well!

YOUR FREE GIFTS!!!

As a big Thank You from us at The Golden Retriever Circle, take this **FREE Golden Retriever Training Cheat Sheet** and **Quick Golden Retriever Training Dos and Don'ts List!**

Visit the link below for more info!

goldenretrievercircle.com/free-gifts/

How would you like to get your next book or audiobook for FREE and get it before anyone else??

Audiobook

Receive your next book or audiobook (and future books) for free each time you leave a review!

Visit the link below for more info!

goldenretrievercircle.com/get-free-books/

LIKE AND FOLLOW OUR FACEBOOK PAGE!

facebook.com/grcircle

To receive the latest news and updates from The Golden Retriever Circle

And Also Join Our Facebook Community!

facebook.com/groups/grcircle

To Ask Questions, Discuss Topics, and Connect with Fellow Golden Retriever Owners

Be sure to check out our other books ***How to Train Your Golden Retriever in 30 Days or Less*** and ***33 Common Mistakes Golden Retriever Owners Make!***

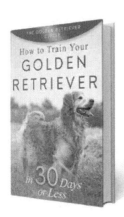
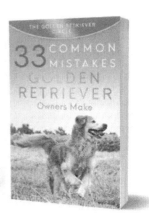

If you want to be known as the **"golden retriever expert"** among your friends and family, these books provide **proven strategies and techniques** to raise your golden retriever.

About The Golden Retriever Circle

Raising your golden retriever doesn't have to be a complicated ordeal. When you take the first step and start training your golden retriever with the very basics, it is actually simple. At The Golden Retriever Circle, we believe that anyone, regardless of dog training experience, is capable of raising a healthy, happy, and well-behaved golden retriever. We are here to provide books and resources to give you a solid foundation on training your goldie.

The golden retriever is one of the most popular dog breeds across the globe. But there are many setbacks that owners face when raising their golden retriever properly. Fear, lack of knowledge and experience, a busy and hectic schedule, the list can go on and on. The Golden Retriever Circle aims to bridge the gap between these setbacks and your goal of raising a healthy and happy golden retriever. Starting with a strong foundation is the only way you can achieve this goal.

We understand the struggle that owners face to find the right approach to master dog training especially for first time dog owners. Our team at The Golden Retriever Circle can help you achieve your goals in raising your golden retriever. Unlike other dog training books and resources out there on the market, our books cater specifically to golden retrievers. Our "circle" is comprised of experts who have a passion for helping people and sharing knowledge especially through our books.

Our team at The Golden Retriever Circle has a passion for sharing their knowledge to anyone who is interested. We write books and resources to give you a solid foundation on training your golden retriever. We firmly believe that anyone, regardless of dog training experience, is capable of raising a healthy, happy, and well-behaved goldie.

You can always rest assure that you are learning from the right people. We look forward to working with you! Because we believe that everyone is capable of raising a golden retriever!

References

Why Do Golden Retrievers Like Water - Wag!. (2019). Retrieved from https://wagwalking.com/behavior/why-do-golden-retrievers-like-water

Perreault, J. (2019). 14 Best Ways To Exercise Your Golden Retriever. Retrieved from https://www.totallygoldens.com/14-best-ways-to-exercise-your-golden-retriever/#Swimming

Top Activities For Golden Retrievers - Wag!. (2019). Retrieved from https://wagwalking.com/activity/activities-for-golden-retrievers

9 Swimming Safety Tips for Dogs. (2019). Retrieved from https://www.goldenmeadowsretrievers.com/9-swimming-safety-tips-dogs/

Five great games and activities to try with your golden retriever | Pets4Homes. (2019). Retrieved from https://www.pets4homes.co.uk/pet-advice/five-great-games-and-activities-to-try-with-your-golden-retriever.html

Everything You Need to Know About Dog Diapers – American Kennel Club. (2019). Retrieved from https://www.akc.org/expert-advice/health/everything-you-need-to-know-about-dog-diapers/

[Breeds] Looking for a low-medium energy dog who enjoys snuggling and lounging as much as occasional hikes. : dogs. (2019). Retrieved from https://www.reddit.com/r/dogs/comments/8e32hg/breeds_looking_for_a_lowmedium_energy_dog_who/

Cold, F., Health, E., Disease, H., Disease, L., Management, P., & Conditions, S. et al. (2019). Urinary Incontinence in Dogs. Retrieved from https://pets.webmd.com/dogs/urinary-incontinence-dogs#2

Urinary Incontinence in the Dog | School of Veterinary Medicine. (2019). Retrieved from https://www.vetmed.ucdavis.edu/hospital/animal-health-topics/canine-incontinence

Urinary incontinence - Symptoms and causes. (2019). Retrieved from https://www.mayoclinic.org/diseases-conditions/urinary-incontinence/symptoms-causes/syc-20352808

Everything You Need To Know About Dog Diapers - My First Shiba Inu. (2019). Retrieved from https://myfirstshiba.com/dog-diapers-all-you-need-to-know/

Jennings, P. (2019). 10 Reasons Why Mental Stimulation Is Important for Dogs - NoHo Arts District. Retrieved from https://nohoartsdistrict.com/all-life/pets-district/item/5598-10-reasons-why-mental-stimulation-is-important-for-dogs

London, L. (2019). Mental Stimulation For Dogs - Keeping Their Brains Busy. Retrieved from https://www.thelabradorsite.com/mental-stimulation-for-dogs/

Golden Retriever Dog Behaviors And Personality traits. (2019). Retrieved from https://www.dogbehaviors.net/golden-retriever-dog-behaviors/

Golden retriever lifetime study sheds light on obesity in dogs. (2019). Retrieved from https://www.fiercepharma.com/animal-health/golden-retriever-lifetime-study-sheds-light-obesity-dogs

Perreault, J. (2019). 14 Best Ways To Exercise Your Golden Retriever. Retrieved from https://www.totallygoldens.com/14-best-ways-to-exercise-your-golden-retriever/

Golden Retrievers and Obesity Issues | Pets4Homes. (2019). Retrieved from https://www.pets4homes.co.uk/pet-advice/golden-retrievers-and-obesity-issues.html

Gaining Weight in Dogs - Definition, Cause, Solution, Prevention, Cost. (2019). Retrieved from https://wagwalking.com/symptom/why-is-my-dog-gaining-weight

Cutts, S. (2019). What Is The Best Food For Golden Retriever Puppies?. Retrieved from https://thehappypuppysite.com/best-food-for-golden-retriever-puppies/

How Much Exercise Does A Golden Retriever Need. (2019). Retrieved from https://www.totallygoldens.com/how-much-exercise-does-a-golden-retriever-need/

Foods to Help Golden Retrievers Lose Weight. (2019). Retrieved from https://dogcare.dailypuppy.com/foods-golden-retrievers-lose-weight-3655.html

Golden Retriever Dog Breed Information. (2019). Retrieved from https://www.akc.org/dog-breeds/golden-retriever/

Made in the USA
San Bernardino, CA
17 December 2019

61694774R00111